HEAVEN ON EARTH AND HOW IT WILL COME

HEAVEN ON EARTH AND HOW IT WILL COME

KATHARINE C. BUSHNELL

WILDSIDE PRESS

BOOK INFORMATION

Published by Wildside Press LLC.
www.wildsidebooks.com

NOTE TO ADULT READERS

My interest in the study of *The Revelation* was first awakened by reading the three-volume work of the Rev. Joseph A. Seiss, D. D. of Philadelphia, USA (not the abridged edition published in London of which he disapproved).

If only this story of mine for young folks will create in them the same interest in the last book of the Bible which the above-mentioned work did in me, I shall be abundantly rewarded though their mature conclusions after close study may differ from mine as much as some of mine do from his.

Someone has said that the only certain interpretation of prophecy is its fulfillment. For this reason, the nearer we get to the time of its fulfillment, the more nearly correct our interpretation should be, other things being equal, of course. I may hope, therefore, that I have shed some light upon the book by the Spirit's aid, which earlier writers could not command.

To reduce this book wholly to symbolism seems to me a positive profanation. Signs and symbols in the book are plainly declared. However, that fact does not warrant the explaining away of its plain and definite statements. And to reduce the book to symbols only is as futile as it is mischievous since it makes an interpretation which no one will accept save the one author of each explanation of that sort.

I am not so eager to win all to my interpretation of each particular point as to create an interest in the earnest study of the book. Also, I desire to convince my readers that the literal interpretation, except where symbols are plainly indicated, is the only useful and legitimate construction that the book will bear. Above all, I want to create an interest and faith in the Lord's second coming.

Should my effort gain encouraging recognition, I shall hope to add some critical comments in the Appendix.

A DEDICATORY LETTER

My Dear Nieces and Nephews,

Not only does an ocean roll between me and my kindred in the United States, but also some of you have grown up into manhood and womanhood since I last saw you. Some of you, I regret to say, I have never seen. Sometimes I need to go over the list afresh to learn the number who has the right of kinship or marriage to call me "Aunt Kate." At present, the number stands close to fifty. I am as proud of my wealth of nieces and nephews as my parents were of the nine children from whom nearly all of you have sprung.

I am writing you sort of a Bible story which relates to a book within it, the study of which is too much neglected; and the only one which contains language such as:

> *"Blessed is he that readeth, and they that hear the words of this prophecy, and keep {treasure up} those things which are written therein."*

It is the only part of the Bible which claims to produce language which has been precisely dictated by the Lord Jesus. Three times over, the Lord testifies personally to its truth, accuracy and authority (Revelation 22:16, 18, 20). He also pronounces the most solemn and awful judgments upon anyone who meddles with its contents, adding or taking from them.

The book reveals to us more about our future destiny in definite terms than any other book of the Bible. Nearly all the contents of the book relate to the events which precede and follow close upon the Second Coming of the Lord. His redemption divides into three parts—to redeem the earth from Satan's rule, to cause "the meek" to "inherit the earth, and to delight themselves in the abundance of peace."

In this book, I shall try to write to you as I love to remember many of you as children clustered about me, waiting for a story. If I forget and my words get too big for you to understand, then the little ones must ask the big ones to explain. When "Grandfather" passed away (my own dear father), his last words were: "Mother, call the children; call them all in." We knew what he meant—children and grandchildren—they were all one to his wandering mind. He wished to give them all his dying blessing. Alas! Though his nine children were all living with their families, only two came to his bedside.

"Grandmother" soon followed him. Along with Grandfather, she always wished, and still does, to call all the children home to them. We used to sing so often at family prayers:

"We are traveling home to God,
In the way our fathers trod;
They are happy now, and we
Soon their happiness shall see."

To me, this song expresses one of the brightest things to which we look forward: That I may live until Christ comes, for the promise is He will bring all our loved ones to rise with us to meet Him in the air as He approaches this earth. They will suddenly appear all about us to accompany us into the Divine presence so that we shall not have to feel so strange and new to it all (I. Thessolonians 4:14). When that time comes, we will undoubtedly feel like singing the other verse of that dear old hymn:

"Lord obediently we'll go,
Gladly leaving all below:
Only Thou our Leader be,
And we still will follow Thee."

In this bright expectation of that for which our parents so often prayed and still pray, "that we may be an unbroken family circle in heaven." I am,

Affectionately yours,

"Aunt Kate"
3 Leicester Street
Southport
October 1914

PART I

A General Survey of "The Day of the Lord"

- John's Vision of the Coming King
- Seven Letters Dictated by the King
- John is caught up to Heaven
- His Vision of a Seven-Sealed Roll
- Six Seals Broken, Revealing:
    (a) A Saving Judgment Agent
    (b) Four Destructive Agents:
        1. War
        2. famine
        3. pestilence
        4. wild beasts
    (c) The Martyrs Demand for Judgment
    (d) The Consummation of Judgment

The Four Destructive Agents Held in Check

- Until 144,000 Jews are sealed.
- These are protected from the Tribulation.
- This "fullness" of the Jews means
- A Resurrection of Christian Gentiles,
- *"Out of the Great Tribulation"* (not yet begun)

CHAPTER I

What "The Revelation" Means
(Revelation 1:1)

People often talk of the last book of the Bible as "Revelations." However, the first thing to notice is that it is called *The Revelation* and tells about one great revelation. Perhaps, you are puzzled because certainly many wonderful visions are described in it. Here we must pause and examine the matter.

Because the book gives an account of many visions which John saw, the natural conclusion is these visions are called "revelations," which gives the name to the book. If such were the case, then the book should have been called "The Revelations of *an Angel*," not "*The Revelation of St. John*"—for an angel showed these visions. John simply wrote them down.

Why could not John's descriptions be called a "revelation"? Someone, at least, thought they could, for he added a second title to the book. How do we know it has two? Because the first one reads, *The Revelation of St. John the Divine;* and we may be sure John would never have called himself "the divine." It would have been very conceited, and John was the most humble and modest of men. His own title begins Chapter 1 and reads: *The Revelation of Jesus Christ, which God gave unto Him.* John is not thinking what a wonderful thing it is to receive revelations or visions. Like Paul, he would not have cared to boast of "visions and revelations." (II. Corinthians 12:1). He had a far grander thought in mind, namely, that Jesus Christ would one day make a wonderful revelation of Himself to the world. Some day, perhaps quite soon now, Jesus Christ is coming to this earth "in the glory of His Father with the holy angels." (Mark 8:38). At that time, God will say to those angels, "Let all the angels of God worship Him."— (Jesus Christ, Hebrews 1:6). This appearance of Jesus Christ on the earth as the King of kings and Lord of lords is John's theme. Jesus, through an angel, showed that second coming of Jesus in a series of wonderful visions; and John wrote them down in this book.

When Jesus came to this earth the other time, He was born as a baby in Bethlehem. He came to win us to love His Father and Himself, and then we would believe on Him and be saved. He came most cautiously so as not to frighten us. We would be afraid of spirits or ghosts if they ever were to appear, which we do not really believe. At any rate, we do not like the idea of seeing a ghost, which Jesus knew. While He was in heaven, He was a spirit. He knew if He came to earth in that form, He would either frighten people away from Him altogether, or else they would be so filled with curiosity at His strange appearance wherever He went. He also knew they would be so eager to ask all manner of questions, He would not have much opportunity to teach them anything useful. They would only want to investigate what a spirit was like.

And besides, He was most holy. The Bible says, "Without holiness no one shall see the Lord," so He could not come to them in spirit form. He must be made over as a man. He was coming "to seek and to save that which is lost," even the most wicked of them. Therefore, He must lay aside all the grandeur of His holy, divine appearance to come among sinners and get them acquainted with Him.

He came in such a way as to get close to them all before they knew who He really was. He came just as every other human being has come into the world. He was born of a human mother. Besides the shepherds and wise men and a few others who saw Him at Bethlehem, the first that knew of Him were the neighbors that said a little baby had come to the sweet, young woman of Nazareth—Mary. Who could be afraid of a *baby*? We laugh at the idea. Next, He was a little boy, playing on the street of Nazareth. Who would run away scared of a little boy? Next, they knew Him as the carpenter's boy, learning his trade at the bench. No one was afraid of the boy who came to do odd jobs about the house to mend a door hinge or a table leg. I am sure the children loved to have Him come because He would allow them to gather close around and ask all kinds of questions about His curious tools. He would never once say, "Now run away, and don't bother Me." One reason for this assumption would be because the children would never feel like troubling Him. Somehow they would feel that they *must* treat Him with real respect.

Like no one else, doubtless He was able to make the children happy; and at the same time not get fretted by their eager questions and bothered into making mistakes in the work. His work would be finished very promptly, and He would be off to the next job, perhaps at the next house.

When He had grown to young manhood, nobody was afraid of Him, for the people of Nazareth had known Him all His lifetime. He looked like quite an ordinary young man except for His very pure, innocent, loving face, even though he shabbily dressed, we think. Though they had always known Him, the rich and proud young men hardly spoke to Him on the Sabbath when He came to the synagogue if He was not able to dress well. Perhaps some of the fine folks, who often talked "business" with Him, snubbed Him when they met Him on the street. All of them would have laughed at the idea of being afraid of a poor, humble young man like Jesus of Nazareth. However, He came especially for the poor who knew and loved Him. Not that He wished to slight the rich, but they would slight Him. Not for Himself would He mind but only for their sakes.

You can see quite clearly that since He was the Son of God, by far He was the greatest man that ever lived. Because He was God at the same time He was man, He was a Mighty Being in disguise. He was God veiled in human flesh. Not that He wished to *deceive* anyone; for just as soon as He became well enough acquainted with anyone to induce that person to believe on Him, He made His real self known. He said He was the Messiah or the Son of God. You will remember when He first met the Samaritan woman at Jacob's well (John 4:25, 26), He told her precisely who He was. He had to take this course in order to get well acquainted with sinners to teach them that He and God the Father loved them in spite of their wrongdoing. Otherwise, they would have felt shy with one so holy.

As you well know in the end despite of all His loving wishes, the rulers of the Jews turned against Him because He rebuked the sins of the hypocrites among them, which caused Him to be arrested and condemned. The Roman soldiers abused Him most shamefully and crucified Him as the Jewish rulers wanted them to do. The righteous wrath of God was so stirred that within a few years, Jerusalem suffered the most dreadful punishment. The Jews had cried, "*His blood be upon us and upon our children,*" and God let it come to pass. After the Jews suffered most frightfully during the siege of Jerusalem, those who lived through the destruction of the city were scattered all over the earth. Almost simultaneously, God sent this word to earth by His Holy Spirit through His servant Paul and recorded in Philippians 2:10-11.

> "*God hath highly exalted Him, and given Him a name that is above every name: that at the name of Jesus every knee should bow, of things in heaven, and things in earth, and things under the earth; and that every tongue should confess that Jesus Christ is Lord, to the glory of God the Father.*"

Since wicked men had so shamefully treated in human courts the holy Son of God as though He were a common fraud and criminal, God declared in the above Scripture His intention to restore Christ's good name and to seat Him on a throne as the Ruler of this entire earth. Every human being in the world would honor Him as king even though up to this time, only a few of millions on this earth acknowledged or believed in Him. It will all be different some day. He will come to this earth surrounded by all the holy angels, who at God's command will worship Him. Hebrews 1:6 says, "When He {God} again bringeth in the firstbegotten into the world, He saith, And let all the angels of God worship Him." Then, will all human beings, too, worship the Son. In this manner will God give glory and honor to Jesus Christ as He now has in heaven and as He had before He came into this world.

Therefore, we know that when Jesus comes again to earth, as He certainly will, He will not come in disguise as the first time. He will not come alone, either. He came alone as a helpless baby the first time. He went back to heaven in a cloud, we are told (Acts 1:9) in the presence of probably over five hundred people (I. Corinthians 15:6). I believe what looked like a "cloud" was really a band of white-robed angels of which two came out of that cloud down to earth and said to the people: *"Why stand ye gazing up into heaven? This same Jesus, who was taken up from you into heaven, shall so come in like manner as ye have seen Him go into heaven."* (Acts 1:11).

Jesus will, then, some day come down to this earth openly out of the sky and attended by a great band of worshiping angels. What a magnificent spectacle this will be for all those who love Him! And what a *revelation* it will be to all those who have never believed He ever lived or that He would ever come back again to earth! John says, *"Behold He cometh with clouds* {crowds of angels}, *and every eye shall see Him, and they also that pierced Him: and all kindreds of the earth shall wail because of Him."* (Revelation 1:7). This reference shows that Revelation which gives the title to John's book. John says again: "The kings of the earth, and the great and rich, the rulers and the mighty men, and every slave and every free man {shall hide} themselves in the dens and in the rocks of the mountains: and say to the mountains and rocks, Fall on us, and hide us from the face of Him that sitteth on the throne, and from the wrath of the Lamb." (Revelation 6:15, 16). This passage describes what the

Revelation of Jesus Christ coming again will be to the wicked—infidels, scoffers, immoral men, blasphemers, murderers, and such, who have cursed His sacred name, be they kings, common men, or slaves. They have never believed they would be punished for their sins, but one day Christ will come suddenly and punish them sorely for their disobedience. Of course, Christians will not be frightened. This truth is THE REVELATION John is going to tell us about, the greatest revelation this earth will ever see.

God promised to give Jesus Christ "a name which is above every name." What is promised and prophesied in the Bible is often spoken of as though past, for with God, no such thing as time exists. We will find many things spoken of as though already past which are yet to come in *The Revelation* as we go on studying the book. Right here, John calls this The Revelation of Jesus Christ which God gave Him though it has not yet come to pass. But what God promises is as good as done.

Some people call the book by its Greek name, *The Apocalypse*, which means "the unveiling" or "the appearing." This Greek word is often used in the New Testament of Christ's second coming. For instance, where we read in our full stop (period) after "Him" in the punctuation of this verse. On the word "gave," read also John 17:24; Psalm 2:8; Philippians 2:9. English Bible, *"When the Lord shall be revealed from heaven,"* the Greek says, "At the *apocalypse* from heaven." (II. Thessalonians 1:7. The same word is used in I. Corinthians 1:7; I. Peter 1:7; 4:13 and elsewhere of the Lord's second coming.

CHAPTER II

A Vision and Letters
(Revelation 1-3)

Next, after his title, John tells us his reason for writing the book, "*to show unto His {Jesus Christ's} servants things which must come to pass swiftly.*" (The original Greek expression as in Luke 18:8 refers to the swift succession of events rather than to their immediate appearance.) When once the time is up and Jesus Christ is about to come, He will come suddenly. Jesus Himself describes that coming as like a thief in the night when no one is expecting Him to come; no one sees the signs of His approach, excepting those faithful ones who are wide awake watching for Him. When He comes to reign on the earth, the preparations for His coming will go forward silently (stealthily, like a thief's coming), and then very rapidly. Exceedingly merciful is it that all will be prepared for Him to take His throne and rule so quickly, for that method means as little suffering on the earth as possible to work such a tremendous change in its control.

Then, John tells us that Jesus sent His angel to show and explain all the visions to him. And because he writes up what he has *already seen*, he writes in the past tense as though it had already happened though it has not. We will also be obliged to describe it this way sometimes as well. You must always remember this point all through our book. We will follow John's plan and often speak as though things had already happened which have not yet taken place. Because John follows this plan, so must we when we are describing John's book.

A blessing is pronounced upon all who study this book. "*Blessed is he that readeth, and they that hear the words of this prophecy, and keep those things which are written therein.*" In early days before printing, books were scarce and dear, and many could not read. Therefore, each church had a "reader" who read the Scriptures to the people. We still have Scripture readings in church services, but such reading is not so important in our day since all have Bibles and can read for themselves. It ought not to be that people should have such difficulty in understanding this book since a blessing is pronounced on those who hear it. Yet, almost everyone who writes commentaries on The Revelation makes a *mystification* rather than a *revelation* out of it.

They seem to think one must know a great deal about history and have a fine education to understand it. However, those who first got the book were not educated people. Every pretended explanation of the book which makes it seem so difficult to understand it to be rejected. The Lord meant that common people should understand Him. Before we get through it, you will find it quite understandable and interesting thanks to learned men like Dr. Seiss, who have given us a clear and natural interpretation of the book.

After the blessing, John says, *"for the time is at hand."* In these days, certain religious teachers talk a great deal about the different "dispensations." With two you will be familiar—the Jewish dispensation and the Christian dispensation. The Jewish dispensation ended when the Holy Spirit descended and filled the early disciples on the day of Pentecost. Since that time, we have lived in the Christian dispensation. When Christ comes, another dispensation will come with Him. The expression, *"the time is at hand,"* means that the Lord's second coming will be the *next* great event on God's program.

The "John" who wrote this book was, of course, the beloved disciple who leaned on Jesus' breast at the last supper (John 13:23). He wrote also the Gospel and the Epistles of John. When he grew old, he lived at Ephesus in Asia Minor. Because of His preaching the Gospel, he was sent into exile to a small island called Patmos, not far from Ephesus. Supposedly, he was working as a slave in some mine on the island when he saw these wonderful visions which were given to tell him in particular what would take place just before and just after Christ's return to rule over the earth. John was sometimes on earth and sometimes lifted up in his spirit to heaven in the visions.

The Holy Spirit took complete possession of him so that he saw things far off in *space* and time. In space, he saw different parts of the earth and heaven often at the same time. In time, he saw that which had not yet come to pass though he saw them eighteen hundred years ago. For example, you discover what John meant when he wrote in verse 10, *"I was in the Spirit on the Lord's day."* "Day" in the Bible often means a long space of time, not simply twenty-four hours. We read frequently of the "day of the Lord." (I. Corinthians 5:5; I. Thessolonians 5:2; II. Peter 3:10; Malachi 4:5; Joel 2:11, etc.) which means a considerable length of time when the Lord comes again to rule or the time of the final period of judgment at the end of all time.

Since John wrote, we have become accustomed to worship on Sunday instead of Saturday as the Jews. Also, we call Sunday "the Lord's day." Rather than meaning, "I was in the Spirit on Sunday," John apparently meant that he was carried forward by the Holy Spirit to the time when the Lord will come to rule on the earth, which is the "Lord's day." John could not have seen all he has written down for us in one single day. Therefore, no point could be made in his saying, "It was Sunday."

His first vision was one of Christ Himself in all His glory as the King. Pause and read it in the first chapter, verses eleven to sixteen. At the end, Jesus Christ Himself explained all its meaning to John. Then, He instructed John to write down three things:

1. *"The things which thou hast seen,"*—that is the vision which John describes here.

2. *"The things which are"* will be described in the letters to the churches in the next two chapters.

3. "*And the things that shall be* {shall come to pass, R.V.} hereafter" or more exactly, "after these things."

John was about to be shown things to be written down at once as they then existed in the different churches as well as things that would take place when Christ should come again. Of course, he did write them down; and they comprised The Revelation. First of all, Jesus dictated seven letters while John wrote them—dictated them just as a business-man dictates letters to his secretary to write out and send off. How very sacred these letters are! Other parts of the Bible tell us about Jesus, but here Jesus Himself does the writing. He writes these letters in the same sense as Paul wrote the epistles. Paul had a secretary to whom he dictated and who wrote his epistles for him. Do you know what proof we have? Search and see. However, these letters are more wonderful than Paul's who wrote his epistles before he died. Jesus died, was resurrected, went to heaven and stayed about sixty years, then came back and wrote these letters through John to the seven churches. These are *most sacred* letters.

Although these letters were meant, first of all, for these particular churches in Asia, they were meant for us too. How do we know? If we did not know it in any other way, we would know it because each letter calls upon everyone who has "*ears to hear*" to listen to what "*the Spirit saith unto the churches*," in those letters. Therefore, as long as ears appear on a person's head, these letters will be meant for that person.

The very contents of the letters show they were meant to cover a considerable period of time until near the time Christ comes again. The first letter threatens, "*I will come . . . and remove thy candlestick*" (2:5). The second one says, "*Be thou faithful unto death*," (2:10), showing they would die before His coming. The third letter contains the threat, "*Repent; or else I will come . . . and fight against them . . .*" (2:16). The fourth letter affirms, "*Hold fast . . . till I come.*" (2:25). The fifth one says, "*if thou wilt not watch . . . I will come on thee as a thief . . .*" and refers to a future church or else it would have said, "if thou dost not watch" (3:3). The sixth letter says, "Behold, I come . . ." {"See I am coming} (3:11). The seventh one declares, "*Behold I stand at the door and knock . . .*" (3:20).

Do you see these churches are each one in time a little nearer to the Lord's return than the church just before in order? More than seven churches in Asia existed when the Lord dictated these letters. Also, churches in Palestine and in different parts of the Roman empire were there because the apostles, particularly Paul, and evangelists had gone all over, preaching the Gospel and founding churches. Since Jesus calls upon all who "have ears to hear" to listen to these letters and because "seven" is the number which means perfection or completeness, these seven churches stand for the complete Church for all time and in all places.

Besides, the name of each church, although it is the actual name of each place to which a letter is sent, describes something in that church to praise or to blame. "Ephesus" means "giving way," and the fault found with this church is they had left their first love. In other words, they had given way to the spirit of the world and did not love Christ as much as they had formerly. "Smyrna" means "bitterness." According to what Jesus tells them in the letter, this church was to suffer the fiercest persecution; and He sends them words of comfort and cheer. "Pergamos" means a "citadel." This church is told, "*Thou dwellest even where Satan's seat is.*" The ruling power of the place was statanic.

"Thyatira" means "unwearied in sacrifices," that is, ceremonies. Although it was a church full of "works," these works were more than their "*charity and service and faith.*" In fact, these works are threatened because of their being mixed with idolatry and uncleanness. "I will give unto every one of you according to your works." (2:23) "Sardis" means "renovation," and this church is told to "*hold fast and repent.*" "Philadelphia" means "brotherly love," and this church is the only one except Smyrna with which Jesus finds no fault. They keep his new commandement, "*Love one another, even as I have loved you.*" "Laodicea means "judgment" or "opinion of the people." This church thinks it is very wealthy, but it is very poor in spiritual things. God has a different opinion from the high opinion it has of itself and says, "*I will spew thee out of my mouth.*"

A beautiful promise is given to those that overcome in the Christian life to each of the seven churches. Because those same promises are given for us as well, we will repeat them:

1) "To him that overcometh, will I give to eat of the tree of life which is in the midst of the Paradise of God."
2) "He that overcometh shall not be hurt of the second death."
3) "To him that overcometh shall not be hurt of the second death."
4) "He that overcometh, and keepeth my works unto the end, to him Will I give power over the nations: and he shall rule them with a rod of iron; as the vessels of a potter shall they be broken to shivers: even as I received of my Father. And I will give him the morning star."
5) "He that overcometh, the same shall be clothed in white raiment; and I will not blot out his name out of the book of life, but I will confess his name before my Father and before His angels."
6) "Him that overcometh will I make a pillar in the temple of my God, and he shall go no more out; and I will write upon him the name of my God, and the name of the city of my God, which is new Jerusalem, which cometh down out of heaven from my God: and I will write upon him my new name."
7) "To him that overcometh, will I grant to sit with me in my throne, even as I also overcame, and am set down with my Father in His Throne."

May God help us all to come oft "*more than conquerors*" through the blood of Jesus Christ. May we obtain the blessedness of all these promises, which would never have been sent to us if they were not well within our grasp.

CHAPTER III

Caught Up To Heaven
(Revelation 4)

We may be sure it was a whole day's work for John to see this first wonderful vision of Jesus Christ in His glorified state and to write those seven letters. Remember, though, he was told that other things to be shown him were to be written down as well as things related to the future. All that follows after chapter 3 relates to those future times after the church has passed through various stages, and Christ stands at the very door knocking close to the time of His second coming.

John begins chapter 4 with, *"After these things I saw, and behold a door opened in heaven . . ."* (R.V.) These words seem to refer to a second vision he had. This time John is taken up into heaven through that open door where he sees things which will happen shortly before the Lord's return. From what is said later on, we may safely state the earliest events as taking place within a few years of Christ's coming. You will remember that He said of the precise time of His return, *"Of that day and that hour knoweth no one, no, not the angels which are in heaven, neither the Son, but the Father."* Also, He said, *"When ye shall see these things come to pass, know that it is nigh, even at the doors."* (Mark 13, 29, 32).

Because He was talking to His disciples, Christ was saying that they need not remain in total ignorance that He is just about to come. On this point, Paul says, "Yourselves know perfectly, that the day of the Lord so cometh as a thief in the night . . . But ye, brethren, are not in darkness that that day should overtake you as a thief." (I. Thessalonians 5:2, 4). Those who believe in the Lord, and are watching for the signs of His return, will know when the time is very near." Many have *pretended* they saw the signs and have falsely heralded His speedy coming. Others have been excited and deluded and have preached He was coming right away when the signs did not warrant any such idea. Others imagine that if they believe in His second coming at all, they much believe and teach that He is coming *right away*, or else they will displease God. Those who have sounded these false alarms are not only wrong, but also they have brought contempt upon God's Word which teaches Christ's return. Such teaching is like the boy who cried, "Wolf, wolf," to often that when the wolf really came, no one believe his cry. Likewise, no one will believe in the glad news that Christ is coming again unless religious leaders of this kind learn to be more careful about what they teach.

Christ *is* coming again, and He is coming suddenly and unexpectedly. If we are not living close to Him and studying His Word carefully, we shall not perceive His coming should it happen in our day. We must not listen to the scoffers who say, *"Where is the promise of His coming?"* You *prove* you did not read your Bibles correctly on this subject "*. . . for* *since the fathers fell asleep, all things continue as they were from the beginning of creation.*" (II. Peter 3:4). Also, do not take your place with those who cry before the time, "He is coming right away!"

Some faulty Christians in Paul's day were misrepresenting his teaching, causing him to write the Thessalonians very calmly not to be "*troubled, neither by spirit (a false prophecy), nor by word, nor by letter from us, as that the day of Christ is at hand*" (coming right away). Then, he goes on to tell some of the signs that must first occur before Christ's coming (II. Thessalonians 2:1-10). To this day, men continue to misrepresent Paul and say he was mistaken because he taught that Christ was coming very soon. Yet, here in his very earliest epistle but one (I. Thessalonians), Paul warns against his being misrepresented on this point.

To return to John, he saw a door in the sky standing open; and a voice bade him come up through it. The Spirit bore his spirit upward until he saw God sitting on His throne in heaven. You can read for yourself the description of how things appeared in the fourth chapter. The one word we regret ever having been translated from the Greek in our English Bibles is the word, "beasts." The word does not say beasts but "living creatures." The Revised Version translates the word correctly. "Beast" is a different word which occurs in a later chapter, describing the Anti-Christ. Just what these four "living creatures" are described in verse 6, we do not know. They seem to be the same as the cherubim Ezekiel saw in a vision (Ezekiel 1) and mentioned elsewhere in the Bible.

Dean Alford thinks they mean, "the whole animated creation" since in the teaching of the Jewish rabbis, the lion was considered the chief of all the beasts of the field. The calf or ox in Ezekiel 1:10 is the chief of the domestic animals, and the eagle is the chief of both birds and fishes who were created on the same day (Genesis 1:20). If John was familiar with this teaching, then these four living creatures very naturally would represent all living things of the animal kingdom. This explanation is the best we know of the "living creatures."

The "twenty-four elders" are evidently human beings who have been redeemed from sin and have gone to heaven, for they sing of themselves as "*purchased unto God*" with Christ's blood "*out of every kindred and tongue, and people, and nation.*" (Revelation 5:8-9).[1] Another thing they sing about gives us a clue why just "twenty-four" are mentioned since they come out of every kindred and tongue and people and nation. The use of the word "elders" often means "representatives." Paul uses the word in its verb form where he says, "*We are ambassadors for Christ . . . We pray you in Christ's stead, be ye reconciled to God.*" These are

---

1   Originally, no warrant existed for changing the "us" and "we" of 5:9, 10 to "them" and "they" except an idea the "four living creatures" of 5:8 presented an obstacle to the former view. It is not necessary to interpret verse 8 so literally as to include them as singers of the song of redemption, but only as prostrating themselves in worship. Dr. Seiss should be read in defense of the A.V. at this place.

ambassadors in God's court, who in our stead are representatives of all redeemed sinners, worshiping before God's throne and praising Him for us.

In chapter 5, these elders say, "Thou . . . hast made us unto our God kings and priests (5:10). The priesthood was divided by king David into twenty-four courses or groups, and these groups of priests served in turn in the Temple (I. Chronicles 24:1-19); Luke 1:5). Since everything in the earthly Temple was a pattern of the heavenly (Hebrews 8:5; 9:23) and since all saints in heaven are "priests" (I. Peter 2:5, 9; Revelation 1:6), therefore, it seems quite natural that the entire body of redeemed saints—many millions—should be represented by "twenty-four elders." They sit on "thrones" because they are more than priests. They are kings as well, and so will we all be who are redeemed by the blood of Christ, *"kings and priests unto God."* To sum up, they are called "elders" because they are mere representatives of millions of redeemed saints. These elders number twenty-four because they represent priests. They sit on thrones because they represent kings as well.

Some Bible scholars think the presence of these "elders" in heaven proves what is called, "the rapture of the saints" (described in I. Thessalonians 4:16, 17) Has already taken place in John's vision. We do not believe it so because that event is described later on by John. You will remember when Christ rose from the dead, many holy, dead people came to life again and some entered Jerusalem and appeared to their friends (Matthew 27:52-53). Again, we are told in Ephesians 4:8 that when Christ ascended into heaven, He *"led captivity captive,"* which means Christ took this released band to heaven with Him. Though these holy, dead people had lived before Christ shed His blood, they must have been redeemed by that same blood since they never could have been actually redeemed in any other way according to the book of Hebrews. (10:1, 4). Also, the book of Acts shows they were redeemed by Christ. (13:39). Therefore, I believe the twenty-four elders were really Old Testament, Jewish saints, but true representatives of a large body of redeemed human beings both in heaven and on earth. We may rejoice, therefore, that we already have in those who praise and honor God and the Lamb of God in our name and for us.

CHAPTER IV

A Seven-Sealed Roll
(Revelation 5)

In the fifth chapter of the Revelation, we read that on the right hand of God John saw a "book." However, we must not think of this book made up of leaves like our modern books. In those days, a book was made of a long strip of parchment or other material rolled up. John saw this type of book sealed with seven seals with something like our sealing wax. The account says that at first no one could be found in the entire universe "worthy" to open the roll. Character, not strength, was needed to open and read the book. No one, neither the apostle John, nor the elders, nor the living creatures, would venture to take the roll from God's hand to open it.

Then, this fact could hardly mean an ordinary book or roll, but rather something in signs or symbols. What does it mean to break the seals and open such a roll? Daniel is instructed (12:4) to "*shut up the words, and seal the book, even to the time of the end,*" which referred to a prophecy that had been uttered. The "sealing" of a book of prophecy means to put the information beyond human knowledge.

When Christ uttered a prophecy about His second coming, He said that no one but God alone knew **when** it would be fulfilled. "*Of that day and hour knoweth no one, no, not the angels of heaven, but my Father only.*" (Matthew 24:36). Again, the disciples once asked Him about the time when the Jews would be restored to their former power as a nation. The Bible declares this event will occur about the time when Christ returns so that if Christ answered the question, they would have known when He was coming again. He did not tell them but said, "*It is not for you to know the times or the seasons, which the Father hath put in His own power.*" (Acts 1:7). The right hand is the symbol of power in the Bible. Up to the time indicated by John's vision, this sealed book, then, contains something which was to remain unknown although it had been prophesied. Further, it was to remain in God's right hand—His power—until the time came to disclose it. Who was to fulfill that prophecy about Christ's return to earth? By His coming, Christ Himself would fulfill it.

John says, "*And I wept much, because no one was found worthy to open and read the book, neither to look thereon.*" On the part of a great, holy man like John, this weeping shows that it was **most important** for the book to be opened.

John knew it was needful to put an end to unutterable misery on earth. As he was weeping, an elder came and comforted him saying, "*Weep not: Look! the Lion of tribe of Judah, the root of David hath prevailed to open the book, and to loose the seven seals thereof.*" This statement sounds as though these seals were put on in a peculiar way. One would be more apt to say, "Loose the seven seals, and open the book." The roll may have been made up of seven pieces. The first piece would be then rolled up and sealed. Then, another layer of parchment wrapped around it and sealed, and so on, until seven layers in all were each sealed. We believe this arrangement was used for reasons which will appear later on in the story.

It seems almost strange that John did not think of Jesus at once, but the elder had to remind him. Was it because He looked so unlike the glorious vision John had of Him in chapter 1? At any rate, the elder called Him the "*Lion of the tribe of Judah*," while John saw Him "*a lamb as it had been slain*." John would remember that when He was like a gentle, loving, non-resisting lamb about to be slaughtered in sacrifice at the Temple, they led Him out and crucified Him. The Lamb had seven eyes and seven horns, which means full spiritual and ruling power. The seven eyes are explained as "*the seven spirits of God.*" Of course, the Holy Spirit is not seven persons, but "seven" gains its meaning from "perfection" or "completeness." John would perhaps remember that in his Gospel he had written the words of John the Baptist, "*God giveth not the spirit by measure to Him*," for the Holy Spirit dwelt in Christ in completeness. As did the elder in Revelation 5, the prophet Isaiah said of Jesus Christ that He was the root of David: "There shall come forth a rod out of the stem of Jesse, and a branch shall grow out of his roots: And The Spirit of the Lord shall rest upon Him, (1) the spirit of wisdom (2) and understanding, (3) the spirit of counsel and (4) might, (4) the spirit of knowledge, and of (6) the fear of the Lord; and (7) shall make Him quick of understanding in the fear of the Lord." (Isaiah 11:1-3). I have numbered the seven qualities which make up the fullness of the Spirit in Christ, which I believe are the "seven eyes" of the Lamb.

The power of a ruler of this world would be represented by a sword, cannon, battleship, or a fort—all invented to *slay* men. From God's standpoint, perfect power is represented as the wisdom of God's Holy Spirit in completeness and by a Lamb that had been slain—not something that *can slay*, but by something which submitted to *being slain*. Jesus had such power over His own spirit that He could let nothing but love flow from it when He wished, even under the most terrible conditions as when the wicked crucified Him. Proverbs 16:32 says, "*He that is slow to anger is better than the mighty; and he that ruleth his spirit than he that taketh a city.*" In John's vision, the time is now close at hand when the earth is to be ruled by the power of self-control and the greatness of wisdom of Jesus Christ Himself. And, those like Him shall rule with Him: "*Blessed are the meek, for they shall inherit the earth.*" May God hasten those blessed days on earth!

Jesus Christ alone had the right character—the "slain lamb" character— to be counted worthy to open this book and break the seven seals. "*And He came and received the book out of the right hand of Him that sat upon the throne.*" "Take" and "receive" are the same word in Greek. It seems more suitable to translate "received" here, for undoubtedly the Father wished to give it to Jesus. You remember how John wrote as the title of this book: "The Revelation of Jesus Christ, which God gave unto Him." I believe we have a picture of that giving. When Jesus receives the book, opens it, and breaks the seals, that is the beginning of that very revelation of Jesus Christ.

When He received the book or roll, a shout arose in heaven: "Thou art worthy to receive the book, and to open the seals thereof: for Thou wast slain, and hast redeemed us to God by Thy blood out of every kindred and tongue, and people, and nation; and hast made us unto our God kings and priests: and we shall reign on the earth (5:9, 10). This message is called "a new song" because when Jesus begins this new work for this world, a completely new order of things will be set up. The Christian dispensation will be finished, and another will begin. At this point, Jesus Christ will begin to break down all the kingdoms of the earth in order to prepare for His own personal government of the world.

This song tells us why Jesus was the One for this task—He is the world's Redeemer. What did "redeemer" mean to John who received this revelation for us? Although the explanation is somewhat long, you will ultimately fully understand how wonderful it is to have a Redeemer in Jesus Christ.

The children of Israel were slaves in Egypt, once. When God redeemed them from slavery, He settled them in the land of Canaan. God did not allow them to take the land, and keep it as they pleased. Rather, He told the people just how they must divide up the land among their twelve tribes. In Joshua 13 to 22, you will find the story. Even then, God only *leased* the land to them, keeping *ownership* Himself. He said to the Israelites, "*The land shall not be sold forever: for the land is Mine; for ye are strangers* (foreigners) *and sojourners with Me.*" One of God's land laws was, "*In all the land of your possession ye shall grant a redemption for the land.*" (Lev. 25:23, 24). For this reason, the Israelites could not sell land outright to each other or to anyone else. At the most, they could only lease it for forty-nine years. The fiftieth year was "the year of jubilee," and a time of great rejoicing because every man's land came back into his possession again. However, if the man who had leased his land died before the year ob jubilee came around, the land returned to his family. Land never went permanently out of one family into another no matter how much might have been paid for it. It was different with the houses in a walled city which had to be redeemed within a year or lost altogether. Village houses, however, belonged to the ground on which they were built.

Because the Israelites inherited their fathers' place on the land from generation to generation and never lost it entirely, the Bible never talks of a man's estates as his "property," but as his "inheritance" or "possession." God was the landowner. Reading on in Leviticus 25, we learn that if a man became very poor and had disposed of his "inheritance" and needed his home, then one of the poor man's relatives should step forward and pay the temporary tenant so much for each year left until the year of jubilee. This payment would represent the poor man's debt to his tenant, and the tenant would be obligated to move at once whether he wanted to or not. In this way, the poor man could return to his land once again. Since God was the landlord over all, He would not allow the rich to become rich by land speculations, nor would He allow the rich to neglect the poor. The men inherited the land except when a father had no sons and his daughters inherited it. In those rough days, much fighting was necessary to defend the land that the men held, which was not required in peaceful lands.

God took care that if the men did hold the land, they could not turn women out homeless. No! A widow who lost her husband and had no son to inherit land for her could demand that if her husband had an unmarried brother, he must marry her.

This nearest male relative was called a *go-el* (pronounced "go-ail," accent on the last syllable) in Hebrew, that is, "redeemer." He had other duties to perform besides putting a poor man back into his inheritance and marrying a sonless widow. For instance, he was the one to slay a murderer if one under his protection was murdered. The poor man thought a great deal of his *goel*. The widow and orphan not only must have thought a great deal of him but also had a right to expect his help

CHAPTER V

A Two-Fold Redemption
*(*Revelation 5 continued)

Some people think the book of Ruth was written merely to tell us some curious and interesting things about the ancestors of David. However, I am sure the book was written mainly to show us a model *goel* and what a comfort such a one could be to a poor, forlorn, homeless family of women. A certain Israelite, Elimelech of Bethlehem, leased his land and went across the Dead Sea into the land of Moab to earn a better living. He had a wife and two sons. In this foreign country, the sons both married Moabite wives. Both the father and the two sons died, leaving three widows sad and poor. Then, the mother-in-law, Naomi, decided to return to Bethlehem. One daughter-in law insisted on going with her, declaring she would renounce her paganism and become a Jewish proselyte. They returned together. By this time, Naomi was probably too old to work. The story tells of Ruth's brave efforts to support them both by gleaning in the fields at harvest time. Where they lived we do not know. However, we may imagine they rented shabby little room somewhere in the village of Bethlehem.

Perhaps you wonder why Naomi did not search immediately for her *goel* and ask for help. In the first place, she was too old to bear a son. Therefore, she could not claim him in marriage, nor could her daughter-in-law who was a foreigner. Israelites did not approve of their men marrying foreigners. The death of Elimelech seems to prove that he did wrong to go and live in a foreign land whereas the death of his sons would be looked upon as God's curse for their having married Moabite women. If this assumption is correct, Naomi would not have the courage to ask for aid at once.

A convert to the Jewish faith, such as Ruth had become, would stand some chance of favor if she proved to be genuine. Ruth, of course, was genuine, When she went out to glean, God Himself seems to have led her straight to the field of her *goel*. Not being a Jewess by birth, she did not understand the *goel* principle. However, Boaz, her wealthy *goel*, did understand. He began to watch and see if she was genuine. Boaz told his field-hands to treat her with all respect and never correct her if in her ignorance she gleaned in places forbidden to other gleaners. They were instructed to pull out handsful of grain to put in her way to glean and to show her other kindnesses. Then, he spoke to Ruth gently and told not to go to any other fields than his to glean. She was told to freely drink the water provided for the field laborers. At times when they were eating, Ruth was invited to eat with them. Boaz offered her food so liberally that she took some home to her mother-in-law (2:18). The goodness of this stranger must have astonished Ruth greatly.

At the end of her very first day, she threshed what she had been allowed to glean and had about fifty pounds to take home! As she continued daily for seven weeks through barley and wheat harvest, we may be sure Boaz continued showing her many kindnesses. At the beginning of the harvest, he told Ruth, "*It hath been fully shown me, all that thou hast done unto thy mother-in-law since the death of thing husband: and how thou hast left thy father and thy mother, and the land of thy nativity, and art come unto a people thou knewest not heretofore. The Lord recompense thy work, and a full reward be given thee of the Lord God of Israel, under whose wings thou hast come to trust.*" (Ruth 2:11). At the end of the harvest, he said to her: "*Blessed art thou of the Lord, my daughter . . . And now, my daughter, fear not; I will do to thee all that thou requirest: for all the city of my people both know that thou art a courageous woman.*" (Ruth 3:10-11).[2]

In time, Boaz performed the duty the law laid upon her as her *goel*, and they were married. When their first child was born (King David's grandfather), the neighbors and friends came and congratulated Naomi, the mother-in-law—not Ruth, the mother of the baby. Does that seem strange? When we understand the custom, it is not so strange. This first son would be recognized not as Boaz' son but the son of Ruth's first husband, Mahlon. Soon, he would leave the home of Ruth and Boaz to live with his grandmother, Naomi, on the land which Elimelech, her husband, had owned before he went to Moab. Boaz must redeem that land and give it back to Naomi for a home before he married Ruth. That is the reason why the neighbors said to Naomi: "*Blessed be the Lord, which hath not left thee this day without a goel* (translated "kinsman"), *that his* (the child's) *name may be famous in Israel. And he shall be unto thee a restorer of thy life, and a nourisher of thy old age: for thy daughter-in-law, which loveth thee (who is better to thee than seven sons) hath borne him.*" (Ruth 4:14, 15).

This reason is why Naomi "*took the child, and laid it in her bosom, and became nurse unto it.*" Boaz was rich and could well have afforded a nurse for the child, but Naomi claimed the child as hers. Then, the neighbors said, "*There is a son born to Naomi,*" though Ruth was the actual mother. This action shows how God refused to leave widows comfortless and alone. Naomi had all the fields of her dead husband back again and a son (though really her grandson) to live with her in her old age to support and care for her.

One part of the story has been passed over almost without mention although it was a matter of great importance to Naomi. *Somebody* was living in Naomi's former home when she returned poor and friendless from Moab. She must have looked frequently with longing to the

---

2   The word "courageous" has been wrongly translated "virtuous" here as though it were needed to defend Ruth from a charge of wrong conduct. Rather, Boaz commends her courage in supporting herself and her mother.

fruitful fields which her husband and his field hands used to reap and to the house where she lived in happy and prosperous days when her husband was alive. Boaz' duty was to pay the tenant for the time left before the year of jubilee so Naomi could return to her former home.

Before Boaz married Ruth, he called the chief men of the town together. According to custom, he said to them: "Ye are witnesses this day, that I have acquired* all that was Elimelech's, and all that was Chilion's and Mahlon's, of the hand of Naomi. Moreover Ruth the Moabitess, the wife of Mahlon, have I acquired* all that was Elimelech's, and all that was Chilion's and Mahlon's, of the hand of Naomi. Moreover Ruth the Moabitess, the wife of Mahlon, have I acquired to be my wife, to raise up the name of the dead upon his inheritance, that the name of the dead be not cut off from among his brethren, and from the gate of his place: ye are witnesses this day." You see, he did not acquire it for himself, but to put someone else there (Ruth's son and his) in Naomi's first husband's home, to be a son to Naomi, and to inherit the dead Elimelech's property, cleared of all debt.

Now, you will understand better, perhaps, what it would mean to a Jew to be told that Jesus Christ was his *Goel*, Redeemer. His *goel* meant his nearest relative, his best friend and powerful patron. His *goel* would be the one bound by law to rescue him if he fell into dire poverty. His *goel* would be the one to care for his widow if he died. Lastly, his *goel* would be the one to avenge his wrongs. Yes, and Christ, our Redeemer, is much more than a *goel* to us.

Before the Lord settled the Israelites in the Promised Land and gave them their possessions, He delivered them out of slavery in Egypt, which became the first part of Israel's redemption. Then, the land was given to them, and a *goel* was provided for each Israelite, meaning he would never lose his inheritance in the land. However, the redemption from slavery came first because it was of no use to give possessions to a *slave*. The owner of a slave owns all the slave has or will have.

At the beginning, God gave us the whole earth as our possession, saying to the man and the woman, "Be fruitful, and multiply, and replenish the earth, and subdue it; and have dominion over the fish of the sea, and over the birds of the heavens, and over every living thing that moveth upon the earth." However, man sinned and came under the power of Satan, becoming his slave. Man's possessions then became the possessions of Satan. Thorns and thistles grew from the ground. Beasts became wild and fierce, and man has been able to subdue only a few of the domestic animals. Snakes and scorpions and other deadly things began to afflict man. The birds and fishes are out from under man's control almost altogether. Also, the land only yields food for man when he works almost like a slave upon it. These situations describe the way Satan has seized man and made him his hard-working slave.

In many places in the Bible, we are plainly told that God's intention is to yet make this earth what it would have been had man never sinned.

First of all, so far as man will allow, He is going to redeem him from Satan's power altogether. Then, secondly, He is going to restore the earth to what it would have been had Satan not marred it and put man back into full possession. You can plainly see that so long as man is Satan's slave, it is useless to give man a redeemed earth.

First, God must have a redeemed people. Then, He can place them in charge of the earth described in Isaiah 11: "*There shall come forth a rod out of the stem of Jesse, and a branch shall grow out of his roots* (that same Root of David, Jesus Christ mentioned in Revelation 5). *And the Spirit of the Lord shall rest upon Him, the spirit of wisdom and understanding, the spirit of counsel and might, the spirit of knowledge and of the fear of the Lord; and shall make Him of quick understanding in the fear of the Lord* (the seven eyes of Rev. 5:6); *and He shall not judge after the sight of His eyes, neither reprove after the hearing of His ears* (that is, superficially): *But with righteousness shall He judge the poor, and reprove with equity for the meek of the earth; and,* He shall smite the earth *with the rod of His mouth* (Rev. 19:15), *and with the breath of His lips shall He slay the wicked* (2 Thessolonians 2:8—Antichrist). *And righteousness shall be the girdle of His loins, and faithfulness the girdle of His reins*" (Rev. 19:11).

Now this work of Jesus Christ, the Redeemer, is fully described in Revelation until Jesus establishes His rule on the earth. In the last two chapters of Revelation, we have a glimpse of the effect of redeeming the earth and giving it back to redeemed man. We will come to the description presently. At this point, we will only write down what Isaiah tells us about it: "*The wolf shall dwell with the lamb, and the leopard shall lie down with the kid; and the calf and the young lion and fatling together; and a little child shall lead them. And the cow and the bear shall feed; and their young ones shall lie down together: and the lion shall eat straw like the ox. And the sucking child shall play on the hole of the asp, and the weaned child shall put his hand on the cockatrice*' (a deadly serpent's) *den. They shall not hurt nor destroy in all my holy mountain: for the earth shall be full of the knowledge of the Lord, as the waters cover the sea.*" What a truly wonderful picture of a redeemed earth!

Perhaps, you are saying, "I will never see the earth this way. I shall be dead and gone to heaven long before that time comes." You are mistaken. When the time arrives, Jesus will come and set up His rule on the earth very rapidly. We are quite likely to live to see much of the above description accomplished, for we do not know how soon He may begin. Should we die in the meantime, we will come back to this earth with Him as superior beings to help in the restoration of the world. We will live here as the rulers of this earth with Him for a thousand years.

I'm getting ahead of the story. John tells us the story, and we shall presently study the details. What I have told you in advance is to whet your interest, for it concerns your personal history if you are a child of God.

First of all, you will understand that Christ intends to redeem *us* from Satan. He cannot redeem the earth and put us back in possession while we are slaves of Satan, for that would merely mean to put our old master—Satan—in charge again. We must not think of ourselves as anything better than slaves of Satan as long as we go on committing sin. It is not so comforting to put ourselves this low when we are sinners.

However, Christ, who is our judge, has put us here. He says, "*Whosoever committeth sin is the servant* (the word means "slave") *of sin*," which is the same thing as being the slave of Satan who provokes us to sin. Everyone who has ever committed a sin has passed under the power of Satan—and that means everybody. Some of us, though, have been redeemed by the precious blood of Jesus, who died on the cross for our redemption. Are you one whom Jesus has redeemed? If not, cry out to Him now to redeem you, and He will hear. He says: "Him that cometh unto Me I will in no wise cast out." So you can be redeemed right now, and become a candidate for a real crown—not an ornament—but a crown that carries with it a right to rule on this earth.

First things come first. We lost our inheritance of the earth because we fell under the power of Satan. What toil and economy it costs a poor man to become the possessor of a few feet of the ground of this earth! The servants of the devil, many being rich men who have made their money dishonestly or who have oppressed the poor, often possess the land under our feet. Likewise, we pay high rent for it instead of having our share free. How did it come about? These men got the land by serving the devil. Remember not all men who have large estates serve the devil. Some are good, of course.

God intends that good people alone shall one day possess this earth. Therefore, He sent His Son to redeem us from Satan that we might come into our possession. When Christ died on the cross to redeem all who would turn to righteousness, was the reason He came *the first time*. We have been at fault in not understanding that Christ is coming a second time *to redeem the earth*. First, He came to redeem *us*.

Next, He comes to redeem our inheritance *for us*. The first time, He redeemed all who will believe on Him by dying for them. The second time, He will *not* be slain for us, but *He will slay* all who will not accept His redemption for their sins. He is "worthy," or the right One, to open the book of judgment on the wicked because He died for them. However, they have gone on despising Him.

He is also the right One to put us in possession of our inheritance of the earth because He purchased[3] us with His own blood. You must never think that Christ purchased us from *Satan*. Christ purchased us from our rightful Owner, His Father. Satan is an unlawful master to

---

3   The word "acquired" should not have been translated "purchased." It does not mean bought, but rather "gotten" (Genesis 4:1). The land could never be sold, nor could Ruth.

whom nothing is due. We have only to tell him in dead earnest, "Be gone!" and Jesus Christ will at once drive him out of our lives.

This entire book of the Revelation has to do with the *second coming* of Jesus to do the *second part* of His work as the world's Redeemer. The first part of His redemption is to redeem *us* from sin, which corresponds to the Lord's redemption of the Israelites from slavery in Egypt. The second part of Christ's work as a *Goel* is similar to the redemption of an Israelite's land.

The "sealed book," or roll in the hand of the Almighty on His throne indicates that the tithe to this earth has always been His and has never passed out of His hand. The time for giving the Jews their land, Palestine, as well as the land itself, are "*in His power*," as Jesus told His disciples. The whole is as a sealed roll because no one knows either the time or the events until God chooses to reveal them. No one has the power to redeem Palestine out of the hands of the enemies of Christ until God the Father gives this power into the hand of His Son. What we say of Palestine is equally true of the whole earth.

In a vision, John saw Jesus Christ receiving this sealed roll. Also, He saw many of the events which follow Christ being revealed as the King of the whole earth, which John wrote down for our benefit. However, the time still remains a profound secret. We can only judge its closeness by recognizing some of the things John described in the Revelation as actually taking place before our eyes. What is God waiting for? He is waiting for sinners to repent so that they need not be punished when Christ comes, even the wicked dead will be raised up and punished in due course.

CHAPTER VI

Six Seals Broken
(Revelation 6)

We say of a good man "His word is as good as his deed." Of God, we must say, "His word is the same as His deed." When God says something has come to pass, He has but one way of working—by uttering His word. "*He spake and it was done: He commanded, and it stood fast.*" Thus, He created the heavens and the earth and everything in them. In that manner, He has ruled all the ages and caused all times and customs to serve His purpose, even the wicked who are in rebellion against Him. When we become wiser, we shall understand although we cannot always see that it is so now.

Jesus Christ is called "the Word of God" by John, the apostle. (John 1:1-4). Also, John tells us in the Revelation that He was called by this name when He led forth the armies of heaven to battle. (19:13). Why is He so called? Anyone who reads His life on earth will learn the will of God precisely as he would learn by a careful study of the rest of Bible, only even more plainly. In fact, the Old Testament was not clearly understood by the Jews, even though they studied it most carefully, until Jesus came and lived on the earth among them. Then, those who believe in Jesus understood with wonderful clearness while those who did not believe on Him became blinder than ever and simply could not understand the Bible.

Jesus Christ *lived out* God's will and became a more perfect revelation than the will as *written out*. In the highest sense, Jesus is God's Word according to God's will. Daniel sealed a certain book of prophecy at God's command. Remember that Jesus Christ is coming back to earth to *live out* the prophecy contained in His apocalypse which names the book, "The Revelation." When Jesus takes the book from His Father's hand instead of *reading out* the words of that book, He is represented by John as *living out* that book. Since Christ chose this method, shouldn't we do the same when we read God's Book—*live out* the words immediately in perfect obedience?

The Lamb, Jesus Christ, opened the first seal and saw His Father's will. As expected, John represents Him as living out that will at once. In a voice of thunder, one of the four "living beings" cry, "COME!"[4] As the representative of some part of animal life on earth (for instance, *humanity*, the Living Being with a human face), this living being did not command Jesus Christ. Rather, he utters the cry of all he represents on earth, including those who are praying most urgently for Christ to come to earth and redeem it and them.

---

4   The added words, "and see," should be dropped from the expression "Come and see" in 6:1, 3, 5, and 7. See R. V.

The living Word of God rides forth on a White Horseman. The "horse" represents power and conquest whereas "white" indicates righteousness and victory. A "bow" means battle and a "crown," victory and rule. Here is illustrated the living word of God going forth in judgment and in a righteous, victorious saving power.

The prophet Isaiah says, "When Thy judgments are in the earth, the inhabitants of the world shall learn righteousness." In John's vision, he sees that as long as these judgments are going forward, some will take warning from them and repent by turning to God. Therefore, He goes forth *"conquering and to conquer."*

Christ, like His Father, is God with the Father. He is not confined to one place. Though He has gone forth in judgment as the Word of God, John sees Him in heaven breaking the second seal. Another Living Being cries, "COME!"

Those animal creatures below the human family know nothing about the saving

judgments of Jesus Christ. The cruelties humans have suffered on earth cause them to cry out for Christ to come. One of those cruelties is depicted in God saying that the blood of Abel cried to Him, making the avenging of Abel's murder a necessity in God's justice. This "COME" is a cry for Christ to avenge wrongs.

WAR stalks forth—red with blood and with a great sword. Peace is removed from the earth. We are reminded of Christ's own words of warning as to what would be a sign of His coming to set up His kingdom on the earth: *"Ye shall hear of wars, and rumors of wars: see that ye* (Christ's own disciples) *be not troubled: for all these things must come to pass but the end is not yet. For nation will rise against nation, and kingdom against kingdom."* The earth had often been disturbed by wars. When these times come, people will say, "It never was so perfectly dreadful in all the history of the world."

Next, come horsemen representing Famine and Pestilence, constant results of wars. One horse is black for famine, and the other pale, a greenish-pale death color. Jesus told His disciples when this time came, *"There shall be famines, and pestilences, and earthquakes in divers places"* (Matthew 24:7). Soon we shall read of some of these earthquakes.

Precisely, what is this vision of the breaking of the seals intended to teach us? I believe it represents the time as having come for Christ to judge the earth. The White Horse teaches us that His judgments will be tempered with mercy and forgiveness for all who will repent under His judgments. Therefore, the White Horseman goes forth before the others are allowed to begin their deadly destruction. The lessons of the other horses are plain in v. 8: *"These were given authority over one fourth part of the earth, to kill with sword* (red horse), *with hunger (black horse) and with death,"* or pestilence (pale or livid horse). Also, we are told that others will be killed by "the beasts of the earth." What a perfectly appalling destruction of life!

Here is a vision of the "powers" the Lord sends forth for the salvation of those who will repent as well as the destruction of the wicked. A horse signifies "power." Presently, we shall see these judgment agents or powers in action.

Famine and pestilence always follow in the wake of great wards. During such times of war, those who conduct themselves like wild beasts will always be present. In conclusion, these scourges are really reducible to one—war—in awful intensity and enormous extent.[5]

What is this "fourth part of the earth" which is to be visited by these scourges? John is looking down from the heavens upon the earth. Naturally speaking, he could see but one hemisphere. He mentions the Euphrates river twice (9:14, 16:12), Armageddon, or the hill of Megiddo in Palestine (Esdraelon), Jerusalem, and "the sea," which would naturally be the one he knew the most about—the Mediterranean. Accordingly, we have traced a map of the eastern hemisphere and divided it into quarters. The northwestern quarter includes all the places John mentions, the heart of which is the Mediterranean Sea situated in the center of the ancient Roman Empire. The Roman Empire which existed in John's day is enclosed in the red lines. In examining the map, study first the map of the hemisphere which is on the right hand of the larger map. The latter is an enlargement of the Roman Empire to which has been added the modern names of countries.

We need not say too explicitly whether John saw all the hemisphere or whether the great wars visit every portion of this quarter of the earth. At least, we may be sure the prophecies of John relate to this portion of the world and to no other. By consulting this map occasionally, you will understand John better.

In breaking the fifth seal, we see the most urgent *demand* for judgment—the cry of martyrs. The four Living beings have uttered their cry for Christ to come in saving or avenging power. Now the cry comes from martyrs represented as souls (their bodies have been killed) under the altar of God. These martyrs are not simply good, dead people, but those who have been sacrificed and killed because they have remained true to God.

The blood of a sacrifice ran off under the altar or around its base in a gutter. Likewise, here the martyrs are represented where their blood ran. They cry as Abel's blood cried from the ground for vengeance. Not that the martyrs cried for vengeance, for their spirit would be one of forgiveness like Jesus when He prayed, "*Father, forgive them; they know not what they do*" or like Stephen when he prayed, "*Lay not this sin to their charge.*" The justice of God cries from their souls under the altar,

---

5   This chapter has *not* been written to suit the striking events of the Great War of the autumn of 1914, for it was written in August 1913. In fact, this entire book was written through chapter 21 before November 1913 although some portions of these chapters have been revised since.

"How long, O Lord, holy and true, dost thou not avenge our blood on them that dwell on the earth?"

The martyrs are each given a white robe. They are told that more martyrs must yet suffer and then God's judgment will fall on those who slew the martyrs. This partial fulfillment is in Revelation16:6.

When John saw the sixth seal broken and the sixth portion of the book unrolled, then a terrible earthquake came with such frightful scenes following. The sun became dark brown and the moon, blood red. Meteors shot through the sky and fell to the earth in vast number. Then, it appeared as though the whole sky doubled up and rolled away. Our imagination cannot fathom such a scene until it takes place. Then, we will understand the description. Such a terrible earthquake occurs that *"every mountain and island moved out of their places,"* and everybody fled in terror, seeking some place of safety. The martyr scene discloses the urgent *demand* for immediate judgment. When the sixth seal is broken, we have a picture of the terrible *results* which will take place under that judgment of Christ. From the kings to the slaves, wicked men will be so frightened that they will call to the mountains and rocks, *"Fall on us and hide us from the face of Him that sitteth on the throne* (God) *and from the wrath of the Lamb* (Jesus Christ): *For the great day of His wrath is come; and who shall be able to stand?"*

CHAPTER VII

A Sealing and a Resurrection
(Revelation 7)

Next, John saw four angels standing *"on the four corners of the earth,"* or as we would say, at the four points of the compass, holding back "the four winds of the earth" from destructive action. About six hundred years before John saw this vision, the prophet Zechariah saw one similar. He saw four chariots with horses, and an angel told him, *"these are the four winds* (the word is translated 'spirits,' but should not have been) *of the heavens"* (Zechariah 6:5). These four chariots with horses undoubtedly mean judgment agents. Therefore, we conclude the "four winds" of our chapter must mean the same thing.

If the "four winds" are judgment agents or forces, it seems natural to conclude that here is another view of the four agents described in 6:8, *"sword . . . hunger . . . death* (that is, pestilence) *. . . the beasts of the earth."* The latter word means "wild beasts" and may refer to military ferocity and human rulers like Antichrist and the False Prophet rather than literal wild animals. However, chapter 13 describes the beast by the same name of "wild beast" as used in chapter 6 as warring with the saints and killing those who would not worship the image of the beast.

We are told that God's angels were keeping these judgment forces or winds from blowing until 144,000 people could be "sealed." This seal is different from the seals on the book in the Almighty's right hand in that it is a mark on the forehead. Those who have traveled in India will understand what is meant. A man puts a mark on his forehead to indicate the religious order or caste to which he belongs. You may have seen this mark in pictures of natives of India.

In chapter 14, we read that the "seal" had God's name on it—"having His Father's name in their foreheads." Do you know what God's name is? "God," do you answer? No, God is His *title*, not His personal name just as "King" is the title of the man on the throne of Great Britain. Likewise, "President" is the title of the man that is head of the American people. However, the king carries a personal name besides as does the president of the United States, and just so does God have a personal name. Do you know what it is? Many scarcely know it. One reason is that the name is almost suppressed in our English translation of the Old Testament. The Jews believe the name is too holy to mention, and the name is only translated a few times. In the rest of the places, the word LORD in small capitals is used instead. If you have an *American Revised Bible*, you discover it immediately. It is *Jehovah*.

The Hebrew word, rather than the English form, will be used because it is the seal on the forehead of 144,000 Israelites. Here is how it would look—

That is the mark they will bear. Those who have this mark will be protected from the judgment winds of war, famine, pestilence and the murderous rulers of that day. This marking was done to teach John, who was to teach us, that God is going to recognize and protect them as His own. God does not need to know them from other people, for He already knows them perfectly. Not only does He know all things, but also He knows that which is yet to come in the future.

When the children of Israel were about to be delivered out of Egypt, the angel of God slew all the firstborn sons of the Egyptians. Also, God required every family of the Israelites to put the blood of a lamb upon the side posts and above the door to guard their firstborn from death. This action was not done to show the angel whom to slay but to teach the Israelites. God wanted them to learn His protecting care provided they would follow all His instructions carefully. Also, God wanted them to learn in advance something about how the blood of Jesus, the Lamb of God, would protect us from judgment. When the 144,000 are sealed, God teaches us how He will care for them.

The peculiar thing to notice here is that they are all Israelites—12,000 out of each of the twelve tribes of Israel. The tribes are mentioned differently from any other place in the Old Testament. The sons of Jacob, or Israel, were Reuben, Simeon, Levi, Judah, Zebulon, Issachar, Dan, Gad, Asher, Naphtali, Joseph and Benjamin. Levi, though, was the priestly tribe. When the Israelites entered the Promised Land, they were not given tracts of land like the other Israelites, but cities and smaller plots of ground. The number was kept at twelve tribes who had tracts of land for farming by dividing the tribe of Joseph into two tribes and naming those tribes after Joseph's two sons, Ephraim and Manasseh.

In this book of Revelation, Levi's name appears again while the tribe of Dan disappears altogether. The tribe of Ephraim is called by the father's name again, Joseph. Why the name of Joseph is chosen, I do not know. Many think Dan is dropped because it is supposed that Antichrist will come out of that tribe with the Danites fighting for Antichrist.

Why will these be sealed and cared for? Either they will have come to believe on Jesus Christ or God knows they will be coverted soon. The Bible says to Christians, "*After that ye believed, ye were sealed with that Holy Spirit of promise, which is the earnest* (pledge) *of our inheritance until the redemption of the purchased possession*" (Ephesians 1:13, 14). From this scripture, we learn that all who believe are sealed.

Zechariah 12:9-14 contains a prophecy of widespread repentance by all families of the Israelites, v. 14. Only four names are mentioned— David and his son Nathan; Levi and his grandson Shimei. These four represent the royal and the priestly lines as repenting, for they are the most important. Then, the rest are mentioned in one body.

It is said: "*They shall look upon Me whom they have pierced.*" First, the spiritual eyes of these Israelites will be opened to realize Jesus Christ as their Messiah. They will also understand that instead of receiving

Him as Messiah when He came, they had Him put to death. After long centuries of blindness, they will finally repent. The, we are told, "In that day there shall be a fountain opened to the house of David and to the inhabitants of Jerusalem for sin and for uncleanness" (Zechariah 13:1).

While we commonly speak of these as "Jews," who are or will be converted to Christ in this period of time, constantly bear in mind this fact: Ten of the tribes of the Israelites were "lost" hundreds of years before Christ. The Jews were scattered to the ends of the earth. God alone knows where some of them are. The word, "Jew," comes from the tribe of Judah. Judah, a large part of Levi, some of Benjamin, and stragglers from the other tribes constitute the body or nation called "Jews" in the New Testament. When converted to Christ, we should call them Israelites as Paul does.

Afterwards, when we mention the Israelites, recall that we are not speaking of the "Jews" merely as we know them. We might think of some of these people who are converted to Christ as American or British or French or German or belonging to some other nationality that has lost their connection with Israel. However, God has not lost their connection. He has watched over them through the centuries until they have been won to Christ. When a sufficient number repent along with those openly known to be Jews, the numbers of each tribe will increase to 12,000. Then, they will be "sealed" and protected from the coming Tribulation which John saw.

Later, in chapters 11 and 12, we learn how these Jews will be won to Christ. Chapter 11 tells about Two Witnesses, one of whom as least, may have been at work winning souls for some time before the 144,000 were saved. One of those Two Witnesses is Elijah. He must have impressed the Israelites tremendously. His chief object in coming to earth again will be to prepare for the Lord's second coming just as John the Baptist prepared for His first coming. Approaching is a great period of winning Israelites to Christ.

Almost every religious movement wins women more readily and in larger numbers than men. Chapter 12 tells us that women will work tremendously in this preparation for the Lord's second coming. Indeed, Isaiah 40:9 commands women to proclaim the Lord's second coming as John the Baptist did His first coming. The verse, however, is obscured by mistranslation and should read: "*O thou woman that bringest good tidings to Zion, get thee up into the high mountain; O thou woman that bringest good tidings to Jerusalem, life up thy voice with strength; lift it up, be not afraid; say unto the cities of Judah, Behold your God! Behold, the Lord God will come with strong hand, and His arm shall rule for Him: behold His reward is with Him, and His recompense* (R. V.) *before Him.*[6]

A prophecy about women preaching is also found in Psalm 68:11, and the Revised Version gives the correct translation: "*The women that*

---

6   More can be learned about this passage towards the end of Appendix C.

publish the tidings are a great host." However, Peter made the matter plainest of all. On the day of Pentecost, he showed that women *must* preach the Gospel or prophesy before the present dispensation closes. He declared that Joel's prophecy about the matter related to the dispensation which began when the Holy Spirit came upon the disciples in Jerusalem when he said, "IN THE LAST DAYS, I will pour out of My Spirit upon all flesh: and your sons and your daughters shall prophesy." Having been addressed to the Israelites, it means sons and daughters of Israel. The sons have already done so, but the daughters have not done so yet. Those daughters must do so, or God's word will fail of fulfillment, which cannot be. Joel continues: "And on My servants and on My handmaidens will I pour out IN THOSE DAYS of My Spirit; and they *shall prophesy*" (Acts 2:17, 18). This last verse refers to women in general, Gentile Christian women who must prophesy before this dispensation closes or God's word would fail to be fulfilled which is impossible.

Notice the words of Scripture in capital letters—"in the last days" and "in those days." Every Bible student knows these two expressions refer to this present Gospel dispensation. Therefore, just as the preaching of men opened the present dispensation, the preaching of women will close it when the prophecies in this direction are completely fulfilled.

Furthermore, as the Gospel was first preached at Jerusalem by Jewish men (the apostles), so will it be when "the women that publish the tidings are a great host." The promise is to the daughters of Israel first and afterwards to women in general. Also, the promise includes the commandment, "*O thou woman that bringest good tidings to Zion . . . to Jerusalem.*" This outpouring of the Holy Spirit will fit the daughters of Israel to proclaim the Lord's second coming in the full power of the Holy Spirit, first at Jerusalem.

Of course, other women have already preached the Lord's second coming with good effect. Not until the Spirit is poured out in full Pentecostal power upon converted Jewesses, however, will Joel's prophecy about women begin to be fulfilled. This outpouring of the Spirit and the work of women, then, will be the chief thing that will win these 144,000 Israelites to Christ so that they are sealed. More will be said when we reach the 12th chapter.

Earlier, we quoted from Zechariah, "*There shall be a fountain opened to the house of David, and to the inhabitants of Jerusalem for sin and for uncleanness.*" No doubt this prophecy is for these same days of which we speak. We see, then, the tribe of Judah, David's tribe, will be the most affected by this spirit of repentance, for the revival will begin among the Jews who have returned to Palestine to live.

The repentance of these Israelites is described by Zechariah: "I will pour upon the house of David, and upon the inhabitants of Jerusalem the spirit of grace (causing them to repent) and of supplications: and they shall look upon Me whom they have pierced, and they shall mourn for Him (Christ whom they pierced) as one mourneth for his only son, and shall be in bitterness for Him, as one that is in bitterness for (the death of) his firstborn. In that day shall there be a great mourning in Jerusalem" (Zechariah 12:10, 11).

When it takes place, we cannot be sure whether the sealing of the 144,000 Israelites means they have already turned to Christ, or that God knows they will shortly repent. At least they are protected by the sealing from the coming Tribulation, which shows they are not under His displeasure as are others. When we come to chapter 12, we will have more to say about this matter. Meanwhile, if you have access to Dr. Adam Clarke's, Bible Commentaries, I advise you to read what he says on the passage in Isaiah 40:9 if you are not yet convinced it relates to women.

After these Israelites are sealed, a description is given of a large body of people "*of all nations, and kindred, and peoples, and tongues,*" standing before the throne of God. These are not Jewish, but Gentile Christians resurrected from the dead. These are not resurrected quite as soon as the 144,000 are sealed. These are not the same saints in heaven mentioned in 5:9,10. Those were in heaven before the opening of any of the seven seals. These "*are coming up out of the great tribulation,*" as verse 14 should have been translated. The Great Tribulation has not actually begun when the 144,000 are sealed. They are sealed while the Tribulation is being held in check so they will not be hurt when it comes. (See Appendix D)

John mentions these people coming up out of the Great Tribulation because their resurrection from the dead is dependent upon the "fullness of the Jews," not because it happens precisely at this time. Paul wrote of this matter in his letter to the Romans. He said that the Jews because they rejected Jesus Christ when He first came had become "blinded," except for a few of them like himself and the early disciples of Jesus. Then, the Gospel went out freely to the Gentiles, who have been accepted by Christ, when they believe. In contrast, the Jews' unbelief was the cause of the destruction of Jerusalem because it led them to crucify Jesus—induce the Romans to do so. This action Paul calls the "fall" of the Jews when he writes, "Through their fall salvation came unto the Gentiles." Then, he adds, "*If the fall of them be the riches of the world, and the diminishing of them be the riches of the Gentiles; how much more their fullness?*"

The fullness, of course, is the 144,000. Then, Paul tells us what this "fullness" will bring to the Gentiles: "*If the casting away of them* (the Jews) *is the reconciling of the world, what shall the receiving of them be but LIFE FROM THE DEAD?*" (Romans 11:12, 15). It is, then, because the conversion of these Jews is reckoned as the cause of resurrection of the Gentiles. It is *not* because this resurrection follows immediately when these Jews are sealed that John mentions the two together. The resurrection is mentioned sooner than it occurs in this chapter.

John says: "After this I beheld, and lo, a great multitude, which no one could number, of all nations, and kindreds, and people and tongues, stood before the throne and before the Lamb, clothed with white robes, and palms in their hand; and cried with a loud voice, saying, Salvation to our God who sitteth upon the throne, and unto the Lamb." (7:9-10). This verse mentions a resurrection of Gentile Christians. They are in heaven with the 144,000 Christ "Jews" still upon the earth, passing through some of the Tribulation scenes but not suffering by them (9:4).

Of the Gentiles, it says, "*These are they who are coming out of the Great Tribulation.*" Some actually teach that this means they are escaping all the suffering of the Tribulation by a translation—not by a resurrection. They seem not to notice what follows. "*They shall hunger no more neither thirst any more*

nor shall the sun light on them, nor any heat. For the Lamb which is in the midst of the throne shall feed them, and shall lead them unto fountains of waters; and God shall wipe away all tears from their eyes"— which proves that they had been through very sore troubles. As to the idea that they have been translated, no translation takes place before the one mentioned under the seventh trumpet, 12:5 after "the second woe is past" (11:14); that is, after the Tribulation is well under way. (See Appendix D.)

PART II

The Tribulation Begins

- The Seventh Seal of the Roll Broken.
- The Prayers of the Saints Loose the Destructive Agents.
- Destructive Agents Controlled by Seven Trumpet-Angels.
- Trumpet One is Blown:
    One third of trees and green herbs are destroyed.
- Trumpet Two is Blown:
    One third of the sea bloody; one third the sea creatures and one third the shipping destroyed.
- Trumpet Three is Blown:
    One third of the fresh waters embittered, destroying human life.
- Trumpet Four is Blown:
    One third of the time, the sun, moon and stars are darkened.
- Trumpet Five is Blown, Bringing the 1st Woe:
    A "Locust" pest prevails five months headed by ABADDON.
- Trumpet Six is Blown, Bringing the 2nd WOE:
    A Great War, destroying 66,000,000 men by fire, smoke and sulphur. (It begins in the Euphrates Valley.)

CHAPTER VIII

All Prayers Are Answered(Revelation 8:1-5)

The last seal is now to be broken and the roll to be entirely opened. The breaking of this seventh seal teaches us how surely and completely God answers prayer. He treasures up every sincere prayer though He does not always answer them as quickly as we might wish. Those prayers of which the answer is delayed are not lost prayers, for they will bring answers at just the right time. When Elisa eth, the mother of John the Baptist, prayed for a son, he did not come at once. She prayed for many years and probably often wondered why God did not answer. In fact, she had become quite an old woman, and her husband, Zacharias, had stopped believing he would ever have a son. We are not told if she had stopped believing, too, but we think not from her beautiful salutation when Mary (the mother of Jesus who was yet unborn) greeted her. It breathes a spirit of faith. Zacharias would hardly believe it when an angel told him he was to have a son, for he asked for a sign that it was true, which displeased the angel Gabriel. (Luke 1:18, 20).

Why did not the son come at once at the natural time instead of after Elisabeth and Zacharias were old people? Actually, God had in mind to send them a greater son than they ever dared hope for. God wanted to send them a son of power and eloquence as well as holiness to do the very great and important work of preparing the way for the Lord's coming. Now off in another village, miles distant from Elisabeth's home, was a young cousin of hers named Mary who had undoubtedly prayed she might have the honor of being the mother of the Messiah, that is, Christ, for whose coming the Israelites often longed.

Also, Mary was a suitable person in her purity of life for God's purpose. We feel sure Mary had repeatedly prayed for this happening to occur, for she was not at all unbelieving when the angel Gabriel appeared and told her she was to give birth to the Messiah. Mary was very young, and Elisabeth was old. How could Elisabeth's son be born at the right time—not too early—to preach the coming of Christ unless Elisabeth was made to wait until Mary grew up to womanhood? So often the answers to prayers are delayed to make them fit in with the answers to other prayers.

Nearly all the prayers described in this chapter are delayed prayers, having been made at various times in human history whose answers will not come until the time set for John's vision has come to pass. In fact, if these prayers could all be done up in a parcel and labeled as to their contents, the outside label would read, *"Thy kingdom come. Thy will be done in earth as it is in heaven."* God's people have been praying the Lord's prayer ever since He taught it to His disciples. Many prayed the same thing before this petition about the kingdom was taught in these words. However, God's will is not yet being done on earth as it is done in heaven. John sees in this vision the beginning of the answer to those prayers, and the remainder of Revelation tells about the completing of the answer.

If we go back to 5:8, we will learn something we passed over to bring in now. Just when Jesus took the roll from the Father's right hand, the twenty-four elders, who represent all God's people, *"fell down before the Lamb, having every one of them harps and golden vials* (bowls) *full of odors, which are the prayers of saints."* The harps represent praise. With praise and thanksgiving, they remind the Lord right at that moment when He takes the roll to break its seals that the prayer, *"Thy kingdom come,"* has been rising from the hearts and lips of saints for centuries. Jesus accepted these offerings of the prayers of the saints for immediate answer. Here in chapter 8:3, we are told that the *"prayers of all saints"* are now to be offered on a golden altar.

Why does it say, "When He opened the seventh seal, there was silence," and it lasted for half an hour? When the first seal was opened, a great cry, "Come," like the firing of a tremendous cannon, came forth. After the second, third and fourth seals were broken—four tremendous reports—the great prayers repeated in the name of all created beings, "Come!" "Come!" Come!" "COME!!"

Next, when the fifth seal is broken, a great, agonizing cry, "How long, O Lord!" Then, after the sixth seal, a terrific explosion such as this world never heard before sounded as though the earth might have collided with Mars or some other body of tremendous size. The earth rocks and reels, the sun turns black, the meteors fly about by the thousands, and everyone screaming runs for shelter. Then, the last seal is broken in the calm of heaven far above all commotion and ruin which John had witnessed on earth. When it is broken, the thousands upon thousands of archangels, angels and redeemed saints, who have been sounding their praises to God are instantly hushed into a profound silence which lasts a full half-hour.

Have you been in a meeting where silent prayer was called for? Two, three, four minutes may have passed, but how long it soon seemed! Did you ever witness an accident when somebody ran for a physician while the rest waited in agonizing, helpless silence? A few moments spent thus seemed an age. Silence of all the angelic hosts—dead silence, while every ear and eye is opened wide in expectation of what may happen next after the terrific things which have already happened. What a tremendously impressive half-hour this time will be!

What is it all for? Just for this reason: All heaven is called to witness HOW GOD ANSWERS PRAYER even though the answer has long been delayed. Every prayer has been treasured up in heaven that has ever been offered from a true heart with the condition, *"Thy will be done,"* in the name of Jesus Christ, our Redeemer.

The scene opens with seven great archangels before God's throne. We know the names of only two of these archangels, Gabriel, who appeared to Zacharias and Mary, and Michael, who is mentioned by both Daniel and John. Daniel mentions Gabriel also. The Jewish rabbis invented fictitious names for all seven, except these two given in Scripture. Next, comes to the front One called "another Angel," who is probably Jesus Christ Himself, for He performs a high priest's part. The only High Priest in heaven or on earth is Jesus Christ, who has been called "the Angel of God's presence" in the Old Testament. He's that same Angel who went with the Israelites through all their wanderings in the wilderness when they left Egypt (Exodus 23:20, Isaiah 64: 9, I Corinthians 10:4).

Christ has a golden censor in His hand with the prayers of the saints the elders offered Him. To these, He adds "much incense," that is, His own merit, and Christ requests of God that the prayers have immediate answer. This action is what we call Christ's intercession as our High Priest in our behalf before God's throne. Here, John sees this intercession, and how it is carried on in heaven.

All true prayers we ever offer to God are answered through Christ's intercession for us after this manner. Some prayers are answered immediately, but other prayers, as we have shown, for good reasons are not responded to at once. Now we see that a time has come in John's vision when all the prayers that have been waiting will be answered along with those just ascending.

Do not misunderstand. Not every request made to God will always be responded to, no matter who makes it. God does not promise to answer any prayer of a sinner but the request for forgiveness that is made in sincere repentance. Besides, we need not expect God to forgive our sins, and thus open the way for an answer to other prayers, unless we forgive others. He taught us to pray, *"Forgive us our trespasses as we forgive those who trespass against us,"* and He said, *"If ye do not forgive, neither will your Father which is in heaven forgive your trespasses" (Mark 11:26).*

People make foolish mistakes, which they would not make if they kept in mind the verse, *"If I regard iniquity in my heart, the Lord will not hear me."* When we excuse ourselves in wrong-doing or try to pass over some wrong we have done and try to forget it, we "regard" iniquity in our hearts. We must repent and make a clean breast of the matter to God and to anyone we have wronged. However, if what we have done lies between us and God alone, we need not confess to anyone but God and not to any human confessor, such as a priest.

I knew a woman in India in fear of the plague when it was raging. Therefore, she prayed and asked God not to let anyone in her family fall ill with the terrible disease. Then, she opened her Bible and read, *"There shall no plague come nigh thy dwelling."* She was very happy and sure they were safe. Within a few days, however, her husband sickened and died of plague. She was fearfully shocked and thought God did not keep His promise. It is not for me to say *for a certainty* why God let her husband die although I did not wonder when I knew these people kept their business running seven days a week. What reason had they to expect God's protection while they were breaking God's Sabbath? Satan can direct our attention to Scripture as well as God. Satan quoted Scripture to Jesus when he tempted Him.

Suppose you promised to pay a man five shillings after he met the conditions you had laid down for his weeding your garden. What if he had begged at your door for the money before he had met half the conditions? You would say, "Away with you. You have not met the conditions. I will not pay you." This woman had not met the conditions to properly lay claim to God's promise. The promise reads, *"BECAUSE thou hast made the Most High thy habitation, there shall no evil befall thee, neither shall any plague come nigh thy dwelling."* She was a Sabbath-breaker that had not made the Most High her habitation.

In pity, God often answers the prayers of those living in sin. When He does so, it is not because they have a right to expect it. The promises in the Bible are for Christians who are living consistently and are trying to please God. Some special promises depend upon the special conditions laid down with them. If these conditions are not heeded, these promises do not bear fruit.

John shows us how God answers these prayers—all the unanswered, properly offered for all time up to the moment of the vision. How did He accomplish it? John sees Jesus taking those prayers in a censor with live coals, adding sweet-smelling incense, representing the merit of Christ's beautiful character and His atonement, and the fire from God's altar picturing God's power and fiery judgments on the wicked. Lastly, He hurled all of it out of heaven down upon the earth. What happened? There came forth *"voices,"* tremendously loud, for John to hear them all the way up in heaven; *"thunderings,"* the loudest noise one ever hears on earth; *"lightnings,"* the most vivid light we ever see; *"and an earthquake,"* the greatest commotion one ever feels or sees on earth.

All heaven, then, is hushed, looks downward, listens, and learns this lesson: Prayer will accomplish more for this world than anything else man can do and carries the greatest power man can ever exercise. "More things are wrought by prayer than this world dreams of," a poet said. However, this chapter in the Bible teaches us that more things are done by God in answer to prayer on earth than by any other means known to man.

CHAPTER IX

The First Six Judgment Trumpets
(Revelation 8:6 – 9:21)

In 2nd Thessalonians (2:6-8), the passage reads as follows in the Revised Version: "Now ye know that which restraineth, to the end that he (Anti-Christ) may be revealed in his own season. For the mystery of lawlessness doth already work: only there is one that restraineth now, until he be taken out of the way (literally, "is out of the way" or "becomes out of the midst"). And then shall be revealed the lawless one, whom the Lord Jesus shall slay by the breath of His mouth." The "lawless one" is Anti-Christ.

Much argument has transpired as to what it is that "restraineth" and the "one who restraineth." For my part, I think we can learn from Colossians 1:16, 17. That which restrains is the presence of the Spirit of Christ in the world; and the one who restrains is Christ. The passage says, *"All things were created by Him* (Christ) *and for Him: And He is before all things, and by Him all things consist,"* or "hold together." Jesus Christ is, to this world what the beams and rafters are to a building. Take them out of the building (if you could), and it would collapse. One of these days, when Christ is ready to judge this world, He will withdraw Himself from this world. No man pulls an edifice to the ground without getting out of the midst of it. Christ will get out of the midst of this world, and then let the world fall into ruins. After that time He will build up a new world free from all wickedness.

Christ's presence in this world in the form of the restraining Holy Spirit is the only thing that keeps wickedness and lawlessness down. Otherwise, the world would be intolerable because men would be far more wicked than they are now. Crime could not be held in check. From the time Christ begins to open that roll by breaking its seals, evil forces were released which also became Christ's restraint — War, Famine, Pestilence and Wild Beasts. However, the loosening of this restraint is gradual.

After these evil forces are abroad, we find them bound (7:1) at the four corners of the earth. Four angels must loose them before they can do harm. Then, later, seven archangel trumpeters arrange among themselves in what order they shall be further loosed. This meaning is seen in the words, *"And the seven angels which had the seven trumpets prepared themselves to sound"* (8:6). In fact, Christ's judgments, which constitute this opening chapter of the Tribulation, are not His invention of trouble for the world. Since the world rejects Him, He will cease from restraining the world from harming itself. He will let wicked men have their own way and work out misery for themselves which *must* result from their choosing their own way unhindered.

His judgment and decision is expressed in 22:11: *"He that is unjust let him be unjust still* (or *"yet more"*)*; and he which is filthy let him be filthy still."* For the present, He will not allow them to plunge headlong into misery. The steps are gradual and regulated by seven angels blowing trumpets.

The destruction works out of their own iniquitous desires as the trumpets free them. In fact, we can trace it all back to that second Horseman—War. They have rejected the Prince of Peace, Jesus Christ, and have founded their nations on the military system. God said to Judah once, *"Thine own wickedness shall correct thee."* So shall it be in the Great Tribulation. Those who will not be corrected by the fruit of their own wickedness and repent, God has doomed to destruction.

The nearer we get to the fulfillment of prophecy, the better we understand it. We can almost surmise what some of these things John describes may mean. In A.D. 96, John, the apostle, did not have human language to describe cannons, motors, airplanes, shots, bombs, and all the rest. The names were not invented until the things themselves were, and none of them existed in John's day. He may have understood precisely all he attempted to describe. John may have had revelation of the very names used in our modern speech. Had he used them, they would not have helped us to understand these things until the prophecy came to completion. Therefore, his descriptions are better than names.

John tells us about the blowing of the first group of four trumpets, which bring the following disasters upon that "fourth part of the earth" shown in our map. The first trumpet looses wickedness, which brings "hail and fire mingled with blood" upon the land. One-third of the trees and grass, every green herb, is destroyed. This destruction is precisely what war does when the land is trampled upon by armies under the "hail and fire" of a storm of bullets and shells. The second trumpet looses war on the sea. Blood and fire do their terrible work until one-third of the shipping and one-third of the fisheries are destroyed.

When the third trumpet blows, John sees the poisoning of the fresh water bodies of the land, which causes a great many to die in consequence. These criminal methods will be resorted to more and more in warfare, for it is impossible to regulate evil.

The fourth trumpet blows differently than all the rest. It brings God's interposition, not another view of the devastating effects of war. The sun, moon and stars fail to give their light for one-third of their due time. God sends a warning of the terrible things that will result if man rushes onward in his wicked career. This foreboding says the very worst part of the Tribulation is just ahead. An eagle flies across the sky, screaming, *"Woe, woe, woe, to the inhabiters of the earth by reason of the other voices of the trumpet of the three angels which are yet to sound" (8:13).* (See R. V.) Of course, this eagle is not an ordinary eagle.

The fifth trumpet sounds, and such a great cloud of "locusts" is loosed on the earth that the sky is blackened. These locusts are not ordinary either, for they sting like scorpions. If the same thing is disclosed in Joel 2, and we are almost sure it is, then these "locusts" are probably warriors. Can this scene portray the use of aircraft for war? If we live until the time prophesied arrives, we shall see. Until then, we cannot be sure. At least, this account describes some form of torture which does not end in death though men long to die to escape it. These "locusts" are like *the scorpions of the earth*" (9:3) and are not ordinary insects. They are an infernal invention that comes out of the bottomless pit. Mark well the king over them (9:11), for we shall hear more of him.

When the sixth trumpet blows, the command is sounded: *"Loose the four angels which are bound at the great river Euphrates."* Please turn to the map and see precisely the location of the Euphrates. When one crosses the Euphrates, one passes into the Promised Land (Genesis15:18). Two hundred million "horsemen and warriors," assemble in this region, for a great battle. However, they do not enter the Promised Land but remain in Turkey or Asia. These four "angels" bound there must be evil angels, for it is not necessary to bind good angels in order to secure the will of God.

A great archangel blows the sixth trumpet and looses these four "angels" of the devil. It seems likely these are those same destructive agents—War, Famine, Pestilence and Wild Beasts. They have not been allowed to operate in this region until a certain fixed month of a certain year at a certain fixed hour of the day and month. The War that has been raging in Europe now passes over into Asia. Lastly, our attention will be centered wholly upon the region around Jerusalem where the nations finally assemble for the great battle of Armageddon.

A tremendous battle will be waged, which will slay *"the third part of the men."* Notice I added a "the" before "men." Although it says so in the original Greek, for some reason "the" is not translated. Surely this interpretation means that one-third of the 200,000,000 men are slain and not one-third of the population of the earth is slain. They are killed by *"fire and smoke and brimstone,"* which implies more infernal inventions. Men use shells, which burst and kill hundreds by their poisonous fumes. Finally, it is announced in heaven that the time arrives for God to *"destroy them which destroy the earth"* (11:18). After this terrible battle, preparations go forward for that task.

PART III

A Mighty Angel Appropriates the Land and Sea

1. HE UTTERS A **LOUD CRY**, WHICH IS KEPT SECRET.

2. HE ANNOUNCES THAT THE MYSTERY WILL BE FIN-ISHED WHEN THE SEVENTH TRUMPET BEGINS TO BLOW.

3. JOHN IS COMMISSIONED TO PROPHESY DURING THIS PERIOD AND ALSO TO MEASURE THE TEMPLE, ALTAR AND WORSHIPERS.

4. TWO WITNESSES PROPHESY FOR THREE AND ONE-HALF YEARS.

5. THEY ARE KILLED AT JERUSALEM AND RESURRECT-ED IN THREE AND ONE-HALF DAYS.

6. THEY HEAR A **GREAT VOICE** SAYING, **COME UP HITH-ER.**

7. THEY ARE TRANSLATED, AND AT THE SAME TIME,

8. A GREAT EARTHQUAKE DESTROYS ONE-TENTH OF JERUSALEM AND 7,000 PEOPLE.

CHAPTER X

THE MYSTERY FINISHED
(Revelation 10:1-11)

In Revelation 9:20, we are told that even after the great battle of chapter 8, none of the wicked left on the earth at that time will repent of the wickedness which has brought so much misery in its train. Their own wickedness will not correct any more. Therefore, from this point, a new method is adopted. Jesus Christ begins immediately to prepare His coming to earth to set up His personal government.

Next, John saw a *"mighty angel"* descending from heaven to earth where John is. The Angel, clothed with a cloud, has a rainbow upon his head. It is said that Jesus will come with a cloud. The rainbow on His head means great glory and power and refers to the rainbow around God's throne (4:3). As his face was like the sun, so was Jesus Christ's face when John saw Him in His glory (1:16). *"His feet as pillars of fire,"* reminds us how John describes Jesus—*"His feet like unto fine brass, as if they burned in a furnace"* (1:15). For these reasons, we think this Mighty Angel is Jesus Himself. John saw Him, but He will not be visible to human eyes when He comes on this errand to earth.

You remember the seven-sealed rolls He alone was "worthy" to open and that He alone died to redeem this earth. This Mighty Angel holds a *"little book,"* a roll, spread open on His hand. I think it is one part of the seven-sealed roll, which contains a description of the boundary lines of the sacred region round about the place of God's Temple at Jerusalem. With that description are the plans of the Temple, and all such things for Jerusalem to be rebuilt for the Lord's reception.

The Mighty Angel cried with a loud voice; but what He said, we are not to know for the present. He said something which echoed like "seven thunders" throughout the whole world. In other words, some great proclamation is made throughout the earth. In Hebrews 12:26, 27, we are told of a time when His voice shook the earth when it was prophesied, *"Yet once more I shake not the earth only, but also heaven."* This verse is probably the fulfillment of that prophecy in John's vision.

The whole world, then, will be thrown into commotion by this voice. People may not know what it means, that is, they may not hear words. However, they will *feel* that something terrible is about to happen. Or, the teaching could be that the "seven thunders" that utter their sounds might be some definite proclamation by heralds all over the world by God's people, who have been made to understand the Lord's message in the last moment that on a certain date Christ will destroy all impenitent sinners on the earth.

If this summation is correct, then we understand why John was not permitted to write down what the Mighty Angel said, which the seven thunders re-echoed. Had John done so, he would have made known when Christ is coming to destroy the wicked from the earth. It is not God's wish for this fact to be known at least not until the time is close at hand.

It does seem as though John was looking upon that time, for the Angel adds to his announcement that, *"There shall be no more delay"* (not "no more time," as the A.V. translates.) This declaration, then, may be God's notice to an undesirable tenant (Satan and his family) that they must vacate. He intends to rehabilitate His kindred—believers—in their own inheritance. Presently, we shall see how Satan and his dupes rise up to resist this ejection and how utterly their resistance will fail.

The Angel plants one foot on the land and one foot on the sea to show He takes possession of both. The God has redeemed the earth, and now He proposes to take possession. No further delay about the matter, for the time will be up when the seventh trumpet begins to blow. Mark the words well as translated in the R.V: *"In the days of the voice of the seventh angel, when he is about to sound, then is finished the mystery of God, according to the good tidings which He hath declared to His servants the prophets (10:7).* "In the days — the trumpet does not give a single blast but blows for a period of many days, we think, for twelve hundred and sixty days or three-and-a-half years (12:6). And that seventh trumpet, or the last trump, will begin to sound the moment *"the mystery of God"* is finished.

What is this "mystery?" Paul, the apostle, also tells us about a certain "mystery," which we will study first. The Jews were a very proud race, especially in Paul's day. They thought nobody was as good as they were and imagined themselves the only people for whom their God, Jehovah, cared. Other nations, who worshiped false gods, claimed to have gods— tribal gods—that belonged to no one but them. The Jews fell into the habit of thinking of Jehovah as a mere tribal god, copying the idea from the idolaters about them. Instead of wishing the entire world to worship Him, for the most part, they wanted to keep Him all to themselves.

When their God came to them in the form of Jesus Christ, they rejected Him and urged the Romans to crucify Him. For this reason, they were sorely punished by God in the destruction of Jerusalem. Since that time, the Jews have been scattered all over the world. Then, the apostle Paul, who was a Jew, was called to preach the Gospel to the Gentiles. They were converted in very large numbers and became Christians. In course of time, these Gentiles were ready to believe that God was their God only and no longer God of the Jews. In this respect, they were as wrong as the Jews before them; for He is the one God of all the earth's inhabitants equally.

Paul, the apostle, frequently warned the Gentiles who had become Christians not to think they were the only people for whom God cared. He said a "mystery" had been revealed to him that the Jews would presently repent and the two bodies of believers, those who were formerly

Gentiles, would become one body in Christ Jesus. We cannot be sure when enough Jews, or "Israelites," will be converted to bring the number up to what God has in mind in order that He will pronounce it "the fullness of the Jews." When that moment comes, the mystery will be "finished." In their dispersion, we have lost track of many of the Jews.

Why was it called a mystery? The reason is not because, as we might suppose, something was mysterious about the matter. The real meaning of the word "mystery" is something which must be explained in order to be rightly understood, not something merely mysterious. The only reason why it is necessary to explain over and over is the selfishness and racial prejudice of men, wishing to believe they are better in God's sight than the rest of mankind. It is something not seen by sin-blinded eyes.

The angel proclaims the mystery as something which God *"declared to His prophets"* (10:7). It is nothing difficult to understand for those who read the Bible carefully, especially the prophetic portions which explain that Christ is to rule over Gentiles as well as Jews. (See Psalm 2.) Paul writes: *"Ye have heard . . . how that by revelation He hath made known unto me the mystery . . . which in other ages was not made known unto the sons of men* (not prophets), *as it is now revealed unto His holy apostles and prophets by the Spirit; that the Gentiles should be fellow-heirs, and of the same body, and partakers of His promises in Christ by the Gospel"* (Ephesians 3:2-6).

Now, do you clearly understand the matter? A great body of Christian believers, Jews and Gentiles, will fully come to some definite number which God has in mind. When that number is complete, then the seventh trumpet will blow. When He was on earth, the Lord said the Gospel must first be preached to all nations for a testimony before the end comes or before the present dispensation closes. Just as Enoch and Elijah were translated, this requirement is in order that this body of believers may be completed and prepared for translation. Then, Christ's fierce punishment will come upon the wicked.

The Reverend Charles Wesley composed a beautiful hymn as a prayer for the Jews. We sometimes hear it sung in church, but how few take in the full meaning of the last verse!

> *"With Israel's myriads sealed,* (Revelation 7:1-8)
> *Let all the nations meet,* (9-17)
> *And show the mystery fulfilled,* (10:7)
> *The family complete."*

The next time you sing the hymn you will understand it better, will you not? We do not know when that seventh trumpet will sound, indicating that "Christ's mystical body" is completely finished to the proper number. However, we do know all true believers in Jesus Christ whether living on earth or "asleep in Christ" will pass through a tremendous experience during its sounding. About that time, such perfectly wonderful things happen all over the world. Being one of the first to be shown some of these things, John describes them before he tells what happens to believers.

John's eyes are directed to Jerusalem and events happening there, for they are the most important of all. Up to this point, he has been shown things in other parts of the world; but now everything centers about Jerusalem. We must bear this fact constantly in mind in order to understand matters clearly.

John has been up in heaven all this time in his visions, looking down upon the earth.[7] He has been there ever since he was called up in Spirit by the words, *"Come up hither"* (4:1). Each vision since has been from the standpoint of heaven, which is John looking down upon the earth.

We are not told with certainty, but it seems most probable that the Mighty Angel, who put one foot upon the land and the other upon the sea, (10:2) took his position on the eastern shore of the Mediterranean. With his left foot on Palestine, God's holy land, John is told to go to this Mighty Angel and take the little book out of his hand, and John obeys. The Angel tells him, *"Take it, and eat it up; and it shall make thy belly (stomach) bitter, but it shall be in thy mouth sweet as honey."*

John took the book and ate it, he says. That sounds curious, for John could not actually chew up and swallow a book. Even we say of a book, "digest its contents." That is what is meant here—John is to digest the contents of the roll, which is handed to him. In other words, he is to read the writing in it until he thoroughly understands and has mastered all its instructions.

John declared that the result was just what the Angel said: It was sweet as honey in his mouth. In other words, when he first read it, he was delighted beyond measure by what it said. However, when he took in the full meaning of all the words, then he found a very bitter sense. Although other Bible students give different explanations and only a few would agree with me, I will tell you what I think it all means. The most reasonable view is that the roll contained a description of the Temple to be rebuilt at Jerusalem. John immediately understood that Christ was coming to the earth again when this event occurred.

The glad news was like honey in his mouth for sweetness. After reading further and pondering, John discovered that he and Elijah were to descend to earth from heaven to prepare the way for Christ's return. John realized that he would endure great personal suffering, which would not be what made John feel that bitterness. What made the book bitter for him to digest would be the terrible judgments that he and Elijah must inflict upon the earth's wicked inhabitants and the terrible doom they must pronounce upon it. This responsibility would be bitterness indeed to John's loving disposition.

---

7   Verse 1 is just as correct if translated, "I saw another Mighty Angel *going* down to the earth."

Up to this point, John has been a silent spectator of all that is taking place in his visions. Now, he must become a part of the visions he sees. He sees himself take the roll, and he hears, *"Thou must prophesy again before many peoples, and nations, and tongues and kings."*

John prophesied, that is, preached the Gospel for many years after Christ was crucified. He prophesied when he wrote his Gospels and epistles. John prophesied when he wrote this revelation of Jesus Christ. In vision, he now is told that he must prophesy yet again before peoples, nations, tongues and kings. His prophesying in the early days of the church was mostly to Jews and more or less local although he went to live at Ephesus in his last days. Here is a world-wide commission being given to John. He will go all over the world preaching, or all these nations will come to Palestine to hear John. John, then, will come with Elijah to this earth to prepare for the Lord's return. Throughout the history of the church, but not in large numbers, good people have believed that John was to be one of the "two witnesses" mentioned in the next chapter. I believe so, too.

I do not know how else to understand this curious place in Revelation where John ceases to be a mere spectator and becomes a part of the vision shown him. Nor, can I understand the word "again" in verse 11 unless it relates to something further than the writing of the Revelation. Otherwise, why should the roll have been so "bitter" as well as so sweet to John?

John had three tasks to perform besides his preaching:

(1) He is to measure and order a space cleared off of 1,000 feet in length and breadth for the Temple to be built. He is to measure, and order cleared off, a space 1,000 feet in length and breadth, to re-build the Temple on. The measurements are given in Ezekiel, chapters 40-43 and 45:2.

(2) He is to measure the altar of incense, which is to be about 4 feet square and six feet high (Ezek.41:22).

(3) And John was told to measure *"them that worship therein."* This seems to mean, to measure off the proper number and the suitable persons to serve in this new Temple.

Such persons are carefully described in Ezekiel 44:9-16, where we read: "No stranger, uncircumcised in heart, nor uncircum*cised in flesh, shall enter into My sanctuary, of any stranger that is among the children of Israel. And the Levites that are gone away from Me* (backslidden), when Israel went astray, which went away from Me after their idols; they shall bear their iniquity... *They shall not come near unto Me to do the office of a priest unto Me, nor to come to any of My holy things, in the most holy place: but they shall bear their shame, and their abominations which they committed... But the priests, the Levites, the sons of Zadok, that kept the charge of My sanctuary when the children of Israel went astray from Me,* *they shall come near to Me to minister unto Me, and they shall stand before Me to offer the fat and the blood, saith the Lord God: They shall enter into My sanctuary, and they shall come near to My table to minister unto Me, and they shall keep My charge."*

Although we cannot understand all of this written before the time, John will evidently understand when the time comes for him to act. As one of those two witnesses, he will "measure" the worshipers and tell who is and is not allowed in the interior of the sanctuary when Christ comes again. Another prophet, Malachi, tells us: *"Behold, I will send My messenger and he shall prepare the way before Me: And the Lord, whom you seek, shall suddenly come to His Temple, even the messenger of the covenant, whom ye delight in . . . And He shall sit as a refiner and purifier of silver; and He shall purify the sons of Levi, and purge them as gold and silver, that they may offer unto the Lord an offering in righteousness."*

This prophecy had an incomplete fulfillment in the purging of the Temple by Jesus Christ when He was here on earth. Its complete fulfillment will occur when He comes again and separates those who are worthy to enter His sanctuary with Him, called "the sons of Zadok" in Ezekiel, and other Levites who can only serve in secondary matters because of their previous fall into idolatry.

CHAPTER XI

The Two Witnesses

(Revelation 11:1-4)

John now sees himself taking an active part in his own vision, for he is at this time an exile on the Island of Patmos. The Mighty Angel, whom he sees in the vision, gives him a rod saying, *"Rise and measure the Temple of God, and the altar, and them that worship therein."* Now, the Temple was not on the Island of Patmos where John was seeing this vision. The Temple was at Jerusalem about six-hundred miles to the southeast of Patmos. Also, this measuring was to take place after that Mighty Angel cried, *"There shall be no more delay"* just before the *"last trump"* sounds, which will wake the dead, and translate God's saints (I Corinthians 15:52). That event has not taken place even though nearly nineteen hundred years have passed since John wrote the Revelation.

What does it mean to "measure the Temple of God?" As a matter of fact, the Temple was not in existence at Jerusalem at this time. What is really meant is the instruction to measure and mark off the ground in preparation for the erection of the Temple and to measure and mark the spot for the altar. In the "little book" given to John by the Angel, he has perhaps a plan of the Temple and its area. John is told to prepare for a Temple according to those plans. It is always the custom, of course, to do such measuring in preparation for the erection of a building.

We must not forget, however, these instructions relate not to something already done but something prophesied in the visions John saw, which has not yet taken place, even in our time. Let us try to imagine what will happen when this vision comes to pass.

Some day, which may be very soon now, we may pick up the morning newspaper in England or America or elsewhere and read of a riot in Jerusalem. The paper will declare that "two fanatics" have appeared on the streets of old Jerusalem and are telling people they must move out of the city or else away to the northern section because the Temple must be rebuilt on a very grand scale.

The people, however, are not willing to believe the Witnesses or to give up their property. Then, it is said, "the fanatics" threaten them even with death if they do not obey. Some are so frightened they give over their property. Later, newspaper reports perhaps say the people have been aroused against the "imposters" and threaten to mob them. The very next edition of the papers may say officers were sent to arrest them and were killed by fire like Elijah of old called down fire upon officers who were sent to arrest him. Then, following will be an account of fearful drought and famine which we will be told that the "fanatics" declare they have procured, as Elijah of old did, as a judgment on the people. More sensational reports may follow telling how man after man has been slain in the attempt to arrest the "fanatics." We shall not know whether to believe the stories told or not.

Perhaps, we shall read at last that the "fanatics" have complete control of the city, and its inhabitants are fleeing in terror of their lives. However, we shall not try to conjecture any more, for no one knows precisely how it will be except God. It may be that at the time the Two Witnesses come to earth, such wide-spread disorder and demoralization is occurring because of the tremendous world war that destroys 66,000,000 souls and is so near that part of the world that no one can learn anything about Jerusalem except those in the immediate neighborhood.

By this time, a large number of Jews will be living in Jerusalem, a "great city" (11:8). Both Jew and Gentile, nearby Bible students on the spot will listen to the preaching of the Two Witnesses and will know the prophecies of the coming of the Two. Also, they will study the evidences and will believe and prepare at once for Christ's coming to the earth. Others will scoff at so "wild" a notion. However, the prophecies of both the Old and New Testaments are very plain on this point. Both Jews and Gentiles know that *"Elijah verily cometh first and restoreth all things,"* before Christ comes just as Elijah came in John the Baptist as his representative the first time Christ came.

John says the "two witnesses" do their work of getting the space measured off for the Temple and their witness-bearing, which they perform in the midst of fearful judgments visited upon those who oppose them.[8]

Although these judgments seem rather dreadful, remember all that has preceded about how God's judgments had already won to repentance all who would yield. Also, we must remember what a fearful state of hardness of heart prevails after the terrible war described in Chapter IX.

The wicked rulers of the land try again and again to arrest and restrain the two witnesses and to punish them for the deaths they have caused through God's co-operation with them in judgments. Each time they try, though, we are told, *"If any man will (tries to) hurt them, fire proceedeth out of their mouth, and devoureth their enemies; and if any man will hurt them, he must in this manner be killed."* Certainly no human being has this power of sending forth fire out of his mouth to kill others. However, God in these men could certainly allow such a fire to spew forth.

As soon as their work is accomplished, then God protects them no longer from their enemies. They become like ordinary mortals, John tells us. Then, a particularly bad ruler, described as *"the (wild) beast that cometh up out of the abyss"* (R.V.), overpowers and kills them. Who is this "wild beast?" Revelation 9:11 tells us his name is Abaddon in Hebrew and Apollyon in Greek. Both of these words mean "Destruction."

---

8   See Appendix A for a summary of reasons for our believing the apostle John is one of these witnesses.

He is a great destroyer, probably some great murderous, military man, like Napoleon. Likely, his feat in destroying the "two witnesses" will bring him his greatest glory. Men will not know that he was able to destroy these two witnesses merely because God ceased to defend their lives when their work was done, and it was in God's plan for them to be killed.

God's own people have believed the Two Witnesses were from Him. Then, imagine their thoughts, seeing the Two slain before their eyes at Jerusalem along with the wicked people rejoicing and *"making merry"* over their dead bodies. Their bodies lie in the street for three-and-a-half days, giving certain proof they are really dead. Some of God's people will be utterly dismayed, believing He has forsaken them. Others will understand the Scriptures better and will only be astonished to see such a wonderful fulfillment of the prophecy here in the Revelation when that time comes.

In vision, John sees the Two Witnesses suddenly come to life again. Then, the wicked are filled with horror and dismay when they see the Two ascending in a cloud that has come down to take them out of their sight. Before they can think further, a terrific earthquake rocks the earth and a large share of the city (*"one-tenth part"*) is destroyed, killing seven thousand inhabitants. Filled with horror, they now exclaim these men were true prophets, and they should have heeded their preaching. Also, they acknowledge God has given them well-deserved punishment for slaying them.

"THE SEVENTH ANGEL SOUNDED" (11:15). This sound is the *"last trump,"* as Paul calls it upon which such tremendous events transpire. Let us turn to his words in I Thessolonians 4:16-18, *"The Lord Himself shall descend from heaven with a shout."* What is that shout? Why, I think it is those words, *"Come up hither" (*Revelation 11:12*).* "With the voice of the Archangel." Have we been told of an Archangel? Yes, in Revelation 10:3, *"He cried with a loud voice, as when a lion roareth: and when He cried, seven thunders uttered their voices." And with the trump of God* (this seventh trumpet): *and the dead in Christ shall rise first: Then we, which are alive and remain (*on the earth)*, shall be caught up together with them in the clouds to meet the Lord in the air; and so shall we ever be with the Lord. Wherefore comfort one another with these words."*

How do we know that the *"trump of God,"* which summons the dead to life and translates God's living people, is this particular seventh trumpet of Revelation 11:15? The reason is the apostle Paul says so: *"Behold, I show you a mystery; We shall not all sleep (in death) but we shall all be changed. In a moment, in the twinkling of an eye, at the last trump: for the trumpet shall sound, and the dead shall be raised incorruptible, and we shall be changed"* (I Corinthians 15:51, 52).

Revelation 10:7 tells us the mystery of God is finished just when the seventh trumpet is about to blow. That trumpet will have been blowing for "days." During that time, Paul tells us the dead rise, living Christians are "changed," and all are caught up together to meet the Lord in the air. When the Two Witnesses are raised from the dead by the voice that says, *"Come up hither,"* the resurrection John speaks of in Revelation 7:9-17 takes place. Also, at the same moment, the sealed 144,000 Israelites are probably translated. In fact, before the prolonged sounding of the seventh trumpet ceases, all God's people, who are ready at the coming of Jesus Christ, dead or alive, will be taken out of the world.

Before we consider this thinking any further, let us turn back to events at Jerusalem. When the Lord comes to set up His rule on earth, His central government must have a far grander place than earth has ever had before. First of all, He ruled His people Israel from the Tabernacle—a tent only about forty-five by fifteen feet in size with a court around it, which was one hundred and fifty feet long by seventy-five feet wide. This Tabernacle was as much as the Israelites could carry about in their wilderness wandering. Then, Solomon built a Temple, exactly double the size of the Tabernacle with a court around it about six hundred feet square. Also, Herod's Temple, the one Christ and His disciples visited often, was about one hundred and fifty by ninety feet in size with porches around it enclosed in an area six hundred feet square, including its outer court. Exclusive of this court, it will be a thousand feet square. John is expressly told not to include its outer court, *"for it is given over to the Gentiles* (nations): *and the holy city shall they tread under foot forty and two months."* (Appendix B.)

As we study the vision more carefully, we see even more. Since God was going to send an earthquake to clear the ground and make it ready for His Temple, the Witnesses were doing a merciful work in warning the people to escape for their lives from that particular region. People perished for their disobedience.

PART IV

The Momentous Seventh Trumpet Begins to Blow

1. Preliminary Announcement of the Program In Heaven.
    a. Preliminary kingdoms of the world become Christ's kingdom.
    b. The Dead are judged.
    c. The prophets, the saints and God-fearing people will be rewarded.
    d. The destroyers of the earth will be demolished.

2. As Preliminary to Rewarding the Good, God Displays the Ark of His Covenant in Heaven.

3. An Interlude for Explanatory Back History.

      The labor of Woman brought the Man-Child to birth. Satan, that Old Serpent, sought to devour her child; but at the call "COME UP HITHER" (see Part III), the child is translated. Under the leadership of Michael, God wages war with Satan, and he and his angels are cast down to the earth. "Having great wrath," Satan turns upon the Woman and upon the "remnant" of the Woman's seed. This event constitutes the third "Woe" which follows immediately the events of 11:13 as 11:14 declares.

4. The Third Woe
    a. Satan turns with great wrath upon the woman, who is borne away into the wilderness.
    b. She is nourished there for three-and-a-half years.

    (Third woe to be continued.)

CHAPTER XII

The Advance Guard of Raptured Saints
Revelation 11:15-12:16)

In heaven, they understand the full extent of the meaning of that seventh trumpet. As soon as it begins to sound, we are told, "There were great voices in heaven, saying, *The kingdoms of this world are become the kingdoms of our Lord and of His Christ; and He shall reign for ever and ever.* And the four and twenty elders, which sat before God on their seats (thrones) fell upon their faces, and worshipped God, saying, We give *Thee thanks, O Lord God Almighty, which art, and wast and art to come; because Thou hast taken to Thee Thy great power, and hast reigned. And the nations were angry, and Thy wrath is come, and the time of the dead, that they should be judged, and that Thou shouldest give reward unto Thy servants, the prophets, and to the saints, and them that fear Thy name, small and great; and shouldest destroy them which destroy the earth.*"

In the events which follow in the next few chapters, we shall see how . . . this heralding of the Divine program is put into execution. Already, the dead of chapter 7 and the Two Witnesses have been resurrected. Now, they are to be judged and rewarded along with all the faithful, resurrected and translated. Next, the wicked will be destroyed from the earth though they will not be resurrected and judged for more than a thousand years.

We come now to the first translation of the saints. During the sounding of the seventh trumpet, all the children of God ready when Christ comes will be taken out of the world. In the interpretation of this twelfth chapter, I do not follow anyone whom I have read. I will give you what I believe the Holy Spirit has taught me. You will find the usual interpretations discussed in Appendix C.

Revelation 11:19 should be read with chapter 12. John then saw "The Temple of God was opened in heaven, and there was seen in His Temple the ark of His testament." The R.V. says, "the ark of His covenant." "Testament" and "covenant" are the same word in Greek which means that God would have all heaven see that He remembers a certain covenant He is about to fulfill. That His power is working to fulfill it as shown by the "Lightnings and voices, and thunderings, and an earthquake, and great hail" which follow.

The twelfth chapter shows the fulfillment of the covenant and must be studied with great care to discover to which covenant it refers.

(1) It is *"a great sign,"* referring to some great covenant.
(2) It related to "woman" or "a woman." Since no word exists for the article "a" in Greek, we can choose either sense.

(3) It tells us about *"that old Serpent"* — the only time Satan is mentioned by this name after Genesis 3:15 except in chapter 20:2.

(4) She brings forth a man child whom he seeks to devour (v. 5).

(5) The Serpent persecutes the Woman.[9] (v. 13)

(6) When the Woman escapes the Serpent, he persecutes *"the remnant ("rest") of her seed"* —all believers.

(7) These are described as believers (v.17).

(8) The man-child, who escapes to heaven, is her seed also but not all of her seed. Hence, all believers constitute her seed.

(9) The "war in heaven" causes Satan to be overcome and cast down to earth by believers. "They over*came him by the blood of the Lamb, and by the word of their testimony; for they loved not their lives unto the death."* They had been mortal once, and they had been redeemed by the blood of the Lamb. Also, they had testified. In the war, they are led by Michael, the archangel

(10) The Serpent is cast down to the earth, losing the exalted position of *"the prince of the power of the air"* (Ephesians 2:2).

Now for the explanation:

(1) The greatest covenant God ever made with mankind was addressed to "that old Serpent," the last time he was mentioned in the Bible, in these words, *"I will put enmity between thee and the woman; and between thy seed and her seed; it shall bruise thy head, and thou shalt bruise his heel."* The learned Canon Payne-Smith once called this: "That promise, of which the whole of the rest of the Scripture is but the record of the gradual stages of its fulfillment."[10] John might well say this covenant with mankind (if the "sign" relates to mankind as we believe it does) was represented to him by *"a great sign."*

(2) And "woman" is the chief figure in this *"great sign."*

(3) And "that" (not merely "the", for we are distinctly pointed back to the last time (Genesis 3:15) Satan was described as a Serpent) *"old Serpent."* The red dragon is next in prominence.

(4) The Serpent is at enmity with the Woman while she is passing through agony such as was prophesied of her (Genesis 3:16).

---

9   To avoid confusion, we will always write hereafter with a capital "W" the Woman of this "great sign."

10   The definite article ("the") indicates a well-known, fixed locality and is not a symbolical "wilderness" as in 17:3 where no article is present.

(5) The Serpent displays enmity towards her seed, the man-child, seeking to devour him.

(6) In the outcome, the Woman's seed overcomes the Serpent.

(7) The head of the Serpent is bruised, and he loses his exalted position as *"prince of the power of the air."*

(8) This bruising is accomplished not simply by Michael but by mortal, redeemed men, or at least had been mortal. (Remove this line underneath!)

From Genesis to Revelation, I fail to find anything in Scripture so completely fulfilled by this "great sign" as Genesis 3:15. As prophesied, the "heel" of the woman's seed was bruised when Christ was crucified. If we follow the Revelation story forward through the next few chapters, we will find it a representation of the process of destroying the Serpent's seed from the earth.

Finally, those chapters show the complete crushing of the Serpent's head. However, more bruising of the heel of the woman's seed will happen besides the crucifixion of Christ. As the learned Dr. Lange says, "According to the New Testament . . . The seed of the woman is not exclusively to be referred to the individuality of Christ . . . according to Paul in Romans 16:20: "the God of peace shall bruise Satan under your feet shortly." That bruising of the heel of "the rest of the Woman's seed" is shown in chapters 13 and 14 under the Antichrist and the False Prophet.

Notice that the old Serpent is represented as "red," indicating war, generally, in this book. We think it does here. By this time, all warfare has passed under the immediate management of Satan.

Now for an explanation of the *"great sign"*: First of all, remember what we have already said about the ministry of women at the end of this dispensation and in the conversion of the 144,000 Israelites. Right here, let me remind you again that by "Israelites" we do *not* mean simply such as you know to be Jews. Those you know are but the remnants of a scattered people.

John says the Woman is *"in heaven."* The same is said of the Dragon or Serpent. We cannot think of Satan in the celestial place where God and His holy angels are where nothing unholy ever enters. Therefore, this reference must mean a spiritual conflict rather than an earthly conflict between Satan and the Woman. The man-child is her *spiritual*, not her physical child. He is born of her *spiritual labor* and sorrow. Every person for whom we labor and bring to Christ is reckoned as our spiritual child. Therefore, we understand this Woman to represent a company of converted women, laboring for the conversion or spiritual birth of others.

"Clothed with the sun" means clothed with the righteousness of Christ. He is the Sun of righteousness. *"The moon under her feet"* seems to mean she has risen above Old Testament light into the New Testament

light of life in Jesus Christ. I think these women must be true Israelites, not Gentile Christians. Her man-child is the 144,000 Israelites.

When we win a soul, we say that convert is a star in our crown. This Woman has twelve stars, one for each of the twelve tribes. She could not very well have been pictured with 144,000 stars. You may wish to know why I believe the child she has represents the 144,000. The thought is not original with me. Others more learned than I have thought so. My reasons can be read in Appendix E.

The Woman's child was to *"rule all the nations with a rod of iron"* (v. 5). For this reason, some have hastily decided this child is Jesus Christ because Psalm 2 says He will rule the world. However, Christ promises this rulership likewise to overcomers (Revelation 2:27). This man-child is precisely described as a body of overcomers in Revelation 12:11.

It is never safe to be too explicit in our statements about prophecy, for the fulfillment of prophecy is its only certain interpretation. What I believe the most reasonable view to be is: Starting with three facts as our basis: First, *"The God of peace"* will *"bruise Satan"* under the feet of believers. Second, the old Serpent is represented as red, the war-god. Third, the believers, called *"the rest of the Woman's seed"* who will bruise Satan, are expressly charged not to fight in these words: *"He that killeth with the sword must be killed with the sword. Here is the patience and the faith of the saints."* (13:10). Beginning with these three facts, then, it seems to me the 144,000 first translated had refused to fight and expected to be killed for refusing. That is the reason it is said of them, *"they loved not their lives unto the death."*

It is reasonable to suppose the spiritual work of that company of women at Jerusalem, remembering that scenes are now being pictured at Jerusalem, not over the whole world. In those days, men were reaping the awful fruits of warfare in the scenes under the seven trumpets, which would put in the very forefront the teaching that Jesus Christ's own example of non-resistance must be followed. In times when war is threatened, we know how men are pressed into enlisting. It is quite enough to say, "Your country needs you." Then, young men must go whether their country is on the right or wrong side in the war. How, then, the war-god would be provoked if 144,000 young men bound themselves together in a Peace Society! Here we see Satan as the real war-god, rising up in his wrath to secure the destruction of this band of followers of the Prince of Peace.

For the most part, woman's influence is bound to be on the side of peace. We can well believe these women of Israel will contend that the men of their own race shall never come into the permanent possession of their Promised Land again except under the banner of Christ as a Prince of Peace. They will remember the promise in both Old and New Testament that *"the meek shall inherit the land,"* to which the Old Testament adds, *"and delight themselves in the abundance of peace."*

Now, we understand why this man-child was taken out of the world and translated to heaven whereas the Woman not translated. Man is the warrior. It is not expected of women to enlist in a war. However, the Woman must be persecuted for influencing men not to fight while Satan would have killed the men if he could have. God has a great calling for the Woman.

Having chosen spiritual, instead of carnal, weapons against Satan, they are translated to a war against Satan of a spiritual sort. Michael and his angels come out to help them, and Satan loses all his power except what he can exercise down on the earth. The whole atmosphere is cleared of his presence. The result is that, a little later, when all the saints are translated, Satan cannot oppose them in the upper regions as he did the 144,000.

Satan, driven down to earth, turns upon the Woman—the women who had been the means of influencing the 144,000 to fight with spiritual weapons only. *"The two wings of the Great Eagle"* bear her away into "the(2) wilderness." The loving Almighty heavenly Father himself (Exodus19:4) bears her away to a place of safety where she is fed and cared for three years and a half *("a thousand two hundred and three score days,"* says 12:6. *"A time, times, and half a time,"* 12: 14, means the same. At the end of this time, she is translated to heaven with all the rest of her seed—Jews and Gentiles.

I think this "great sign" is that to which Paul, the apostle, refers but not precisely to the sign which he never saw, rather to the facts taught by it. When he says of woman: *"She shall be saved through the childbearing, if they* (women) *continue in faith and love and sanctification with sobriety."* (R. V.)

The lady's sister told me of the wonderful deliverance her sister had in San Francisco after the great earthquake and fire. Aged and alone, she found herself homeless in a burning city, and she could see no means of escape. Suddenly, she *felt* her dead father on one side of her and her dead brother on the other. She did not see or speak to them, nor did they see or speak to her. They guided her over heaps of rubbish, ankle-deep in dust between fires in round-about ways.

After miles of walking under the greatest difficulties, she came without weariness to the Ferry which took her across the Bay to Oakland. A friend took her in gladly. Her garments were so fresh that all they needed was brushing. Only the residents of Oakland and other cities round about San Francisco, who took refugees from the doomed city and attended to their needs, were able to appreciate what a miracle such freedom from weariness, heat, dust and grime implied. I am reminded of this incident when I read John's account of how holy women will be carried away from scenes of the great tribulation *"on two wings of the Great Eagle"* and sheltered and fed in a safe place.

John went back in his story to the work of these women in the conversion or spiritual birth of the Jews. Then, he went forward through the three years and a half those women are taken care of in the wilderness. What point in this sign of the Woman and these events of chapter 12 corresponds to the time of the events of chapter 11 where John broke off? It is very easy to join the time of the two chapters. John has taken care of that matter. In 11:14, we read, *"The second woe is past; and, behold, the third woe cometh quickly,"* or to express it in common speech, "Look! The third woe is coming right along!" That third woe is described in chapter 12 in these words, *"Woe to the inhabiters of the earth and of the sea, for the devil is come down unto you, having great wrath, because he knoweth that he hath but a short time."*

A voice had called, *"Come up higher . . . and the same hour was a great earthquake,"* after which the third woe came on quickly. Then, it looks as though that great city that raised the two witnesses probably translated the 144,000 also. These fought their way through to heaven with the help of Michael, who came to meet them. The result of the battle was that Satan and his angels were cast down to the earth. Then, Satan turns upon women because of the good work they have accomplished, sending a flood (which may signify an army) after them. God carries them away to a place of safety. Then, Satan turns all his attention to the Christian men in Jerusalem, who are at his mercy for a short season.

PART V

The Closing Events Under the Seventh Trumpet

1. Satan Turns Upon the Rest of the Woman's Seed.
2. He Raises up Antichrist for This Purpose
3. And the False Prophet.
4. Warning Sounded Against Christians Going to War.
5. Christ with the 144,000 Descend for the Rescue of Christians.
6. An Announcement that the 144,000 are the (early) firstfruits.
7. Angelic Warning Against the Worship of Antichrist.
8. Angelic Warning, "Babylon is fallen."
9. Angelic Warning Against "*the mark of the Beast.*"
10. THE SON OF MAN APPEARS ON A CLOUD AS A HAR-VESTER.
11. An Angelic Call for the Harvest to be Reaped.
12. THE EARTH IS REAPED by the SON OF MAN.

(This reaping constitutes the later firstfruits.)

CHAPTER XIII

The REIGN OF ANTICHRIST
(Revelation 12:17–13:18)

When the Woman escaped the dragon, he turned upon *"the rest of her seed"* who remained within his reach. This seed is known by two facts: They *"keep the commandments of God,"* and *"have the testimony of Jesus Christ."* Later in 19:10, we are told *"the testimony of Jesus is the spirit of prophecy."* Hence, we conclude that these whom Satan turns upon are testifying that Christ is coming soon in judgment upon the earth, and He will translate all His saints into His presence. Satan now tries to turn their testimony into a trap for their souls.

He goes and stands upon the sand of the sea. (It should be translated "he stood" not "I stood.") This place of standing was probably the beach of the Mediterranean near Joppa. We must understand that John is still being shown matters in the region of Jerusalem and nowhere else. We do not know what will be taking place all over the world after chapter 9 except for an occasional glimpse now and then. Indeed, some think that from first to last the entire book of the Revelation describes the state of things in Palestine alone or its immediate neighborhood.

John says, "I saw a beast rise up (coming up) out of the sea, having seven heads and ten horns, and upon his horns ten crowns, and upon his horns ten crow*ns, and upon his heads names of blasphemy."* This word for "beast" means a wild beast. It is altogether different from the word used for the "four living beings," but translated unfortunately "beasts" in the Authorized Version. John sees the creature as a wild beast, for he sees through his false professions in the blasphemous names on his head, such as in all probability "king of kings and lord of lords," titles that would be blasphemous for him to assume according to his real character, which is beastly. To ordinary, unspiritual eyes this creature will seem very lovely—the most splendid and gifted and powerful of men. After all, he is the man who is going to rule for a short time at Jerusalem as Antichrist—Christ's great enemy and counterfeit.

Satan usually tries to imitate God's work and to produce his skillful imitation just before God's work appears. He induces men to answer their own prayers instead of waiting for God to answer them at the proper time. As a consequence of what Abraham and Sarah did, Ishmael was born before Isaac, the child of promise. To this day, the Ishmaelites are a troublesome lot for the inhabitants of Palestine. Herod built the Temple for the Jews just before Christ came. He wanted to be considered the Jews' Messiah even though he was not a real Jew, but an Ishmaelite—an Idumean. The men of his party, the Herodians, were persistent persecutors of Jesus Christ. Herod was a type of the coming Antichrist as was Nero. John pictures the actual Antichrist, not a type.

The Two Witnesses had prophesied that Jesus was coming again, and all in the world must be ready for Him. The "seed of the woman" believers were doubtless preaching the Second Coming all over the world. Then, they learn that not only have the Two Witnesses been slain and translated but also a large body of women has disappeared from Jerusalem and perhaps in other places as well.

However, these women have not been translated yet, only hidden from the coming fury of the beast. A large number of men, the 144,000, were translated. We imagine this might make them very uneasy. They would remember the Lord's words: *"Then shall two be in the field; the one shall be taken, and the other left. Two women shall be grinding at the mill; the one shall be taken, and the other left."* (Matt. 24:40-41). With so many in their midst missing, they might begin to fear they were left behind. If so, this state of perplexity would afford Satan the best possible opportunity to deceive God's people.

What it means when Satan calls Antichrist up from the sea, we are not certain. Yet, when he appears, he has been wounded with a sword-thrust (13:12, 14). This wound killed him, and now he is alive again. Later, we are told that he *"shall ascend out of the bottomless pit"* (17:8). This time, however, he does not ascend from there but out of the sea.

In 11:7, we are told that the one who slew the Two Witnesses was *"the beast that ascendeth out of the bottomless pit,"* making him alive on earth at the same time of the Two Witnesses. For these reasons, we believe when the "beast" slays the Two Witnesses the people will see them rise again from the dead. Remember, these are the same people who made merry over the death of the witnesses. Also, when they feel the terrible earthquake, these same people will turn and take vengeance upon the "beast" and slay him with the sword, throwing his body into the sea. Satan, then, will resurrect him to life again.

Can it be possible Satan should ever have such power? Yes, quite possible, for Paul prophesies this very Antichrist's *"coming is after the working of Satan, with all power and signs and lying wonders (2* Thess.2:9). And, it is certain the people recognize this "beast" as someone they knew before. Also, they recognize him as someone whom they knew to have been killed, for they are all filled with wonder because he is alive again (13:3). As we understand it, Antichrist is the same "beast" that slew the Two Witnesses. In the meantime, he has been killed. Now John sees him come up out of his watery grave as the Apollyon in 9:11.

Now, just imagine what perplexity must fill the minds of uninformed people who do not know their Bibles. When the Two Witnesses were slain and came to life again, they were sure that proved they were genuine. Those Two Witnesses turn upon the "beast" that killed them and slew him. Now, that "beast" comes to life again.

Alas! *Who* is genuine, and *whom* shall they believe? Now they cry, *"Who is like unto the beast? Who is able to make war with him?"* The "beast" takes advantage of their perplexity and fright and makes all manner of blasphemous boasts that he is Christ, who has come in judgment to put down all his enemies. He begins *"to make war with the saints, and to overcome them."* And the world gives him complete rule over its entire length and breadth.

However, God's own intelligent people will not acknowledge him. Therefore, he persecutes or slays them, for they have no power to resist him. At this time, God causes good people to resist all temptation to try to fight against this monster. From this time forward, all military action is forbidden to God's people. They are commanded to let Antichrist do his worst, and resistance will be punished by God. The message goes forth: *"If any man have an ear, let him hear. He that leadeth into captivity shall go into captivity; he that killeth with the sword must be killed with the sword . . ."* (13:9-10).

From the time of that battle in heaven when Satan was cast out into the earth, it was announced by a loud voice in heaven: *"Now is come salvation, and strength, and the kingdom of our God, and the power of His Christ"* (12:10). From this point on, Christ assumes the right alone to rule. Either by putting wrongdoers in prison or waging war against them, those who attempt to rule will be punished by Christ. He alone will put down the wickedness of the world, after which His saints will rule with Him.

"Here is the patience and the faith of the saints," ends verse 10. This statement means that because Christians may not even try to defend themselves from Antichrist's violence, both their patience and their faith will be sorely tried. Often we hear it said that Christians should prefer above everything else to live to be translated when the Lord comes. Yet, a higher glory is possible for those who live until near the time when Christ comes and who accept a defenseless death under Antichrist. These martyrs will make up the full number which will hasten the Lord's coming (6:11), and they have special mention and honor when Christ comes to establish His rule on earth (20:4).

About this time, Satan brings another "beast" up out of the earth, who comes out of an earthly grave much like the first one came out of a watery grave. We are not told whether people see where he comes from, but he becomes the head of a great religious organization. This man will work with all his might to secure obedience and worship of the first "beast." He is mild and lamb-like in appearance, but his speech is Satanic. He is called the *"the false prophet"* in 16:13, 19, 20, and 20:10. Therefore, we will call him that from the first. Now, we have fully developed a diabolical trinity—Satan, the counterfeit of God; Antichrist, a counterfeit of Jesus Christ; and the False Prophet, counterfeit of the Holy Spirit.

Satan knows the Bible as well or better than we. He quoted Scripture to Jesus Christ to tempt Him. Satan is a very pious fraud. All he does is imitate God. Whenever he can, he finds out what God is about to do and then hastens to make a fraudulent copy of God's work to impose on us as the real work of God which has been promised. We have a Christ raised from the dead who showed the wound print in His side to Thomas.

Satan produces his Antichrist, who is also raised from the dead, and has a wound print to show. Christ is called the one *"who is, and who was, and who is to come"* (Rev. 1:8), and it is said, *"They that dwell on the earth shall wonder* (and worship), *whose names were not written in the book of life . . . when they behold the beast that was, and is not, and shall come"* (17:8, RV). As it has been prophesied, *"At the name of Jesus every knee should bow, of things in heaven, and things in earth, and things under the earth; and that every tongue should confess that Jesus Christ is Lord"* (Phil. 2:10-11). Therefore, as far as possible, Satan sees to it that all are compelled to worship his false christ. The False Prophet carries out his will at this point.

The False Prophet makes an image of Antichrist and causes it to speak. and he does it so skillfully that, with something in the image like breath, some of the people are convinced that the image has been created and brought to life by the False Prophet. The false miracle succeeds. Most of the inhabitants become idolaters and worship the image. Those who will not are boycotted and can neither buy nor sell. In time, they will starve in unless God rescues them.

Meanwhile, Antichrist will enter a temple built at Jerusalem and will establish his throne. From there, he will rule and be worshiped in person. Likewise, his image will be worshiped. Paul tells us about Antichrist seating himself in God's temple for worship and pretending he is God. (2 Thessalonians 2:4).

Imitating the two witnesses by bringing fire down from heaven, the False Prophet compels the people to make images like his breathing and talking image and to worship those images (13:13). Those who will not worship the image of Antichrist will be killed. Others will be marked in their right hand and forehead as worshipers of the beast, boycotting and starving those who will not yield. These events will transpire probably during the entire three-and-a-half years Antichrist continues to rule (13:5). What sad, sad times these will be for God's people who live in the midst of these trials!

If only they will study their Bibles diligently, especially the Revelation, God's people need not be deceived as to Antichrist when he comes. We may not understand all that is in the book until the time comes. As a learned writer has said, "The only certain interpretation of prophecy is its fulfillment." It is not meant that we should understand every prophecy before its fulfillment. However, we should understand enough that when it begins to be fulfilled, then we will be able to identify it because of our familiarity with the Scriptures.

Now, a very curious method of discovering Antichrist by his very name when he comes is told us. The method did not seem so strange in the days when John wrote it because the Jews were in the habit of using it for other purposes. In early days, the letters of the alphabet in various languages were used for figures. This method remains to this day in the Roman numbers we use on the face of clocks or for chapters of the Bible, for example. Although not true of Roman numbers, generally speaking, a=1; b=2; c= 3; d=4, and so on. Antichrist is merely a title that John gives him (I. John 2:18, 22; 4:3). However, the sum of the letters which make up the name of Antichrist is 666.

Do we know any name that will equal this sum? Yes! Either in Latin, Greek or Hebrew, many names will, but we are not told in which language to compute the name. Some of the names proposed are: Nero, Diocletian, Luther, Calvin, Napoleon, Balaam and Caesar. The oldest interpretation on record is given by one of Polycarp's disciples—Irenaeus, A.D. 170, who was one of John's disciples. Irenaeus declares the name is *lateinos*, meaning "Latin." In Greek, L = 30 + a = 1 + t = 300 + e = 5 + i = 10 + n = 50 + o =70 + s = 200 with the sum total of 666.

It so happens that the Greek letters for the phrase, "the Latin kingdom" (*he basileia latine*) also equal 666 as well as the Hebrew word for Roman—*romith*. Probably, this solution is correct, especially since other strong reasons exist for believing Antichrist will be of the Latin race. But, we have already spoken of Antichrist being a Jew from the tribe of Dan. That tribe, however, is not mentioned in chapter 7. Also, the obscure prophecy in Genesis 49:17 causes us to leave the matter in uncertainty for the present.

As to the False Prophet, it is not unlikely that some day in the future a so-called "Reunion of Christendom" will take place. However, according to the present trend, all "religious" faiths, pagan and Christian, will be taken into it. Should this circumstance ever happen, the Pope of Rome is the only one upon whom all are likely to agree for the head of that Reunion. Then, he may prove to be the False Prophet who will persecute all who will not worship Antichrist. Others teach, however, that Antichrist will be a Pope of Rome.

CHAPTER XIV

The Defense and Translation of God's Saints
(Revelation 14:1-16)

God's people had no need to defend themselves. John could see what was not visible to mortal eyes—the Lamb, Christ Himself and the 144,000 with Him, standing on (or just above,[11] in the air) Mount Zion. Christ was ready to remove them instantly from the power of Antichrist and the False Prophet as soon as it was in God's plan to end their keen sufferings. The case was just as in the day Jesus Himself was arrested. When Peter would have defended his Master with his sword, Jesus said, sternly, *"Put up thy sword into its place; for all they that take the sword shall perish with the sword."*

Then, He said to Peter, "Thinkest thou that I cannot now pray to my Father, and he shall presently give me more than twelve legions of angels? But how then, shall the Scriptures be fulfilled, that thus it must be?" So it will be in the days of Antichrist. Certain Scriptures are to be fulfilled, but rescue will come in the very instant all has been fulfilled. A Roman legion in Christ's day numbered about 6,000. More than 72,000 angels were hovering about Him to defend Him.

Also, twice 72,000 (144,000) will defend God's servants from Antichrist; and the King of Kings will be their Captain. This thought should abundantly comfort those called upon to stand defenseless as far as visible arms can be seen in the presence of the persecuting False Prophet when Antichrist is ruling on earth. Nothing can overtake them but what their heavenly Father permits.

The account tells us these 144,000 are uncommonly holy men, who had never been mixed up with any uncleanness when they were on earth before translation (14:4). Also, they are Christ's own special attendants, for they *"follow the Lamb withersoever He goeth,"* and they are also *"firstfruits unto God and to the Lamb. And in their mouth is no guile: for they are without fault before the throne of God."*

God taught the children of Israel many lessons by means of the Temple services, especially as related to future events of importance for them to know.

He established feasts and fasts for them to celebrate. Three times a year every Hebrew male had to go up to Jerusalem to attend feasts. A clear account of these requirements is given in Deuteronomy 16.

(1) The feast of the Passover and of Unleavened Bread lasted eight days. Women often attended, but no explicit mention is made

---

11 The preposition translated "on" bears the interpretation "above," which means the more likely position of the Lamb and the 144,000.

they were expected. At this feast, the *first* firstfruits offering was made which consisted of a sheaf of grain (Lev. 23:10).

(2) The Feast of Weeks lasted one week. It was later called the Feast of Pentecost because it came just fifty days later. On the fiftieth day after the first firstfruits offering of a sheaf of grain, a *second firstfruits* offering was made, consisting of two leavened loaves of wheat bread (Lev. 23:17). This second feast anticipated women would be present as far as possible. (Deut. 16:11).

(3) Again, the women were expected to attend, as far as possible, the Feast of Ingathering at the end of the civil year (Deuteronomy 16:14). This feast celebrated the ingathering of all the harvest fruits and lasted seven days. The people spent their time in booths made of branches of trees, etc. It was also called The Feast of Tabernacles, and celebrated the wilderness life of the children of Israel (Lev. 23:39-43).

All three of these feasts had to do with harvest times. Other feasts were also celebrated—the Feast of Trumpets, the Feast of Purim, The Feast of Dedication and the Day of Atonement. Now, we are interested only in the three feasts which had to do with harvesting in the signs and visions John describes. This harvesting of the world will follow the outline laid down by the feasts appointed by God and to be celebrated by the Israelites.

In Revelation 14:4, the 144,000 with the Lamb are stationed somewhere in the air above Mount Zion, *"were redeemed from among men, being a* (not "the" as translated) *firstfruits unto God and unto the Lamb."* These, then, answer to the *first* firstfruits. They are "from among men" because they are scattered Jews gathered from every part of the world. With no women expected to be present, this offering is of men and is represented in Revelation 12:5 as a man-child.

In his *Introduction to the Holy Scriptures*, the learned Dr. Horne tells us how a number of priests would go into the fields and reap a handful of the first-ripe grain at the beginning of harvest time before any grain had been reaped . "These, attended by great crowds of people, went out of one of the gates of Jerusalem into the neighboring corn-fields. The firstfruits thus reaped were carried with great pomp and universal rejoicing through the streets of Jerusalem to the Temple . . . These firstfruits, or a handful of the first-ripe grain, gave notice to all who beheld them that the *general* harvest would soon be gathered in." This early presentation of a mere handful of grain as contrasted with a later presentation of two loaves of bread baked from the newly reaped, winnowed and ground grains of wheat prefigured the translation and presentation before God's throne of the 144,000 Israelites, as contrasted with a latter translation of the general Christian body made up of both Jew and Gentile saints (Revelation15).

Again, let me say that probably no mortal eyes saw the Lamb and the 144,000. Had God's tried people, whom the False Prophet was threatening with death if they did not worship Antichrist, seen these holy defenders, they would not have needed the warning which is now sounded: *"I saw another angel flying in mid-heaven, having the everlasting gospel to preach unto them that dwell on the earth, and to every nation and kindred, and tongue, and people"* (14:6). John still had his eye on events around and in Jerusalem, but he knows this message goes to the ends of the earth. *"Saying with a loud voice, Fear God, and give glory to Him* (not to Antichrist), *for the hour of His judgment is come: and worship Him that made heaven and earth, and the sea, and the fountains of waters."* (14:7). Again, we do not suppose this angel was seen by mortal eyes. It probably means that at this time God's people everywhere the world over are stirred by this heaven-sent messenger to give this warning.

Next, a warning goes forth as to the morally fallen state of Babylon or Jerusalem under Antichrist as we shall show presently. Then, a third message follows: *"If anyone worship the beast and his image, and receive his mark in his forehead, or in his hand, the same shall drink of the wine of the wrath of God which is poured out* (chapter 16 pictures this wrath*) without mixture* (not mingled with mercy*) into the cup of His indignation; and he shall be tormented with fire and brimstone, in the presence of the holy angels, and in the presence of the Lamb."* (14:10). This statement means in the presence of the seven wrath-angels, who pour out the vials of God's wrath a little later.

In Revelation 6:16-17, the period is described as the time of the "wrath of the Lamb." *"Here is the patience of the saints: here are they that keep the commandments of God, and the faith of Jesus"* (14:12). What it means is, "Here is a chance for God's people to show how much patience they have and how much faith that God will avenge their wrongs." From this time, the persecution becomes so terrible for Christians that death is preferable to life: *"Blessed are the dead that die in the Lord form henceforth,"* says a voice from heaven (v. 13). Perhaps it is also meant to encourage Christians to go to martyrdom gladly since God will bless them in some special way just as indeed 20:4 shows that God will. *"Yea, that they may rest from their labors; and their works follow with them"* (RV, v. 13). They are rewarded for these "labors" by a thousand years of reigning with Jesus on the earth.

When things come to such a pass, we may be sure Christians will not be left to suffer long. And, so it is, for John next sees Jesus, the Son of man coming to earth on a cloud. *"On His head a crown, and in His hand a sharp sickle."* He comes and reaps the earth. When Jesus was taken up to heaven in a cloud, it was promised, *"This same Jesus, which is taken up from you into heaven, shall so come in like manner as ye have seen Him go into heaven."* And, Paul tells us: *"We which are alive and remain shall be caught up . . . in the clouds, to meet the Lord in the air"* (I. Thessolonians

4:17). This event takes place when Christ reaps the earth. Next, we shall see these *second* firstfruits presented to God on the sea of glass before His throne.

PART VI

I. CHRIST'S JUDGMENT SEAT

The Reward of the Righteous:
    Presented as the second *Firstfruits to God*.

The Punishment of the Wicked:
    (a) Its culmination, as the Treading of the Winepress
    (b) Its details, as the Vials of Wrath, poured out:
        Vial One: A Painful Sore.
        Vial Two: A Bloody Sea.
        Vial Three: Bloody Rivers and Springs.
        Vial Four: A Scorching Sun.
        Vial Five: Darkness and Agony on "The Seat of the Beast."
        Vial Six: Assembling for Armageddon, Drying of Euphrates.

II. INTERLUDE

A Final Warning to God's Deceived Children to be Ready to Escape Babylon
    Vial Seven: Armageddon.

III. DESCRIPTIONS OF BABYLON

CHAPTER XV\

CHRIST'S JUDGMENT SEAT
(Revelation 14:17 to 15:4)

At once, another reaping follows: "And another angel came out from the altar, which had p*ower over fire; and cried with a loud cry to Him that had the sharp sickle, saying, Thrust in Thy sharp sickle and gather the clusters of the vine of the earth; for her grapes are fully ripe.*" Like grapes gathered together into a great winepress to be trodden upon by the Almighty, the wicked will now be destroyed. An eastern winepress was similar to an open-air, shallow basin scooped out of the ground. Then, its floor and sides were cemented. Into this basin, bunches of grapes were thrown upon which the men trod with their bare feet.

Speaking of this same judgment time, Isaiah 63:1-4 says, "Who is this that cometh from Edom, with dyed garments from Bozrah? This that is glorious in his apparel, traveling in the greatness of his strength?" And the Lord answers: "I that speak in righteousness, mighty to save." Then, the prophet asks: "Wherefore art thou red in thine apparel, and thy garments like him that treadeth in the winevat?" The Lord answers: "I have trodden the winepress alone . . . for I will tread them *in my anger, and trample them in my fury; and their blood shall be sprinkled upon my garments, and I will stain all my raiment. For the day of vengeance is in my heart, and the year of my redeemed is come.*"

The King's Winepresses were just outside the wall of Jerusalem in the King's Garden in the Kidron Valley (Nehemiah 3:15, Zechariah 14). A most terrible battle will take place at Armageddon of which we will learn more presently. The blood of the slaughtered men and animals will be up to the horses' bridles in the deep valley outside Jerusalem, and the stream of blood will extend along a distance of 160 miles northward and southward. From Bozrah in Edom to the south to the plain of Esdraelon, or Megiddo, from which Armageddon gets its name, this terrible battle will be even greater than the one described in 9:15. In that battle, 66,000,000 people will perish; but it will be the last battle this earth shall ever see. Does it seem impossible to you that blood should ever flow so deep as horses' bridles?

Murray's Guide to Syria and Palestine relates regarding the town of Bether, which is about six miles to the southwest of Jerusalem, as the place where the Jews under *Bar-Choba* made their last stand against the Romans in the time of Hadrian (A.D. 135). The siege lasted three-and-a-half years. When the city was captured, 800,000 persons were slain. The horses waded up to their bridles in blood. Rivers of blood along the streets were so strong they carried away stones weighing four pounds. Thousands of Jews were taken captive and sold as slaves under the oak of Mamre. Yet, this story is only profane history, which may be exaggerated. The Bible, however, does not exaggerate. We have no conception whatsoever of the terrible bloodshed of this great battle of Armageddon when it takes place. The entire history of this world has never furnished anything to which it can be compared. The greatest slaughter will be at that point in the deep Kidron valley known as "the king's winepresses."

Romans 14:10 says, "we shall all st*and before the judgment seat of Christ.*" Beginning in Revelation 15, we are taught about this judgment. John begins with these words, "And I saw another sign in heaven, great and marvelous, seven angels having the last seven plagues; for in them is filled *up the wrath of God.*" Presently, He will show us in more detail what was meant by the trampling of the grapes in "the great winepress of the wrath of God."

Suddenly, John recalls, or seems to recall, that he is getting ahead of his story. Those grapes will be gathered together, but they will not be trampled upon just yet. Not until God's prepared children—those ready for translation—are taken out of the way, judged before Christ's judgment seat, and presented before God's throne as the *second* firstfruits offering.

Although no description is given of them being taken out of the world, we have Paul's words elsewhere: "Behold, I show you a mystery; we shall not all sleep, but we shall all be changed. In a moment, in the twinkling of an eye, at the last trum*p: for the trumpet shall sound, and the dead shall be raised incorruptible, and we shall be changed*" (I Corinthians 15: 51-52). Again, he tells us: "The Lord Himself shall descend from heaven with a shout, with the voice of the archangel, and with the trum*p of God: and the dead in Christ shall rise first. Then we which are alive and remain, shall be caught up together with them in the clouds,* (Christ descends, sitting on a cloud, Revelation 14:14-16) to meet the Lord in the air: and so shall we ever be with *the Lord.*" (I. Thessalonians 4:16-17)

God's translated children have been judged as to their faithfulness as Christ's servants and rewarded according to their use of the talents entrusted to them during their Lord's absence from the earth. John next calls attention to their presentation before God's throne: *"And I saw as it were a sea of glass mingled with fire: and them that had gotten the victory over the beast, and over his image, and over his mark, and over the number of his name standing on the sea of glass, having the harps of God. And they sing the song of Moses the servant of God, and the song of the Lamb, saying, Great and marvelous are Thy works, Lord God Almighty; just and true are Thy ways, Thou king of saints. Who shall not fear Thee, O Lord, and glorify Thy name? . . . for Thy judgments are made manifest"* (15:2-4.)

Next, we will see these judgments are made manifest as to the wicked. Before we pass on to them, we ask why does it say that these sing both the song of Moses and the song of the Lamb?" The reason is that both Jew and Gentile Christians are now united in one body. The firstfruits offering, which represented them in the ancient Temple offerings, were two loaves of leavened bread (Leviticus 23:17).

Since the coming of Elijah, one of those Two Witnesses, to restore all things, Gentile Christians understand and value Moses and his law and the entire Old Testament as never before. And, since the prophesying of John, the other of the Two Witnesses, the Jewish Christians understand the New Testament and believe it. They see how it explains and completes the Old Testament. Therefore, in full accord, the two bodies now united as one sing both of Moses and of the Lamb.

Moses composed a song when the children of Israel came through the Red Sea on dry ground. That same water piled up on either side, letting them pass through, came together again and drowned the Egyptians pursuing them. These have just escaped the fury of Antichrist and the False Prophet, as they did of old Pharaoh and his host. So we think they sing the song composed by Moses on that occasion: *"I will sing unto the Lord for He hath triumphed gloriously"* (Exodus 15:1).

And, then, they sing the song of he Lamb. Perhaps this song is the one in 5:12-13: "Worthy is the Lamb that was s*lain to receive power, and riches and wisdom, and strength and honor and glory, and blessing . . . Blessing, and honor, and glory, and power be unto Him that sitteth upon the throne, and unto the Lamb for ever and ever."*

The second firstfruits were offered at Pentecost in the New Testament (Acts 2:1). On that day, the Holy Spirit descended in power upon the disciples (men and women) assembled in the upper chamber. According to Mosaic law, as previously stated, it was customary for women as far as possible to attend this feast (Deuteronomy 16:11). This quickening of the living disciples of Jesus Christ at Pentecost prefigured the quickening leading to translation of those who are alive at His coming.

Let us repeat: This general translation included both Jewish (aside from the 144,000 Israelites before mentioned) and Gentile Christians. The presentation before God's throne of these two classes of people in one body was prefigured by the *second* firstfruits offering of the Levitical law (Revelation 15:2, Leviticus 23:17). This offering consisted of two loaves of leavened wheat bread and came after, and not before, the grain had been reaped and made into flour. The *first* firstfruits offering was merely a handful of the grain called a "sheaf," which was cut from standing barley before it was reaped. Fifty days spanned the offering of the two firstfruits. The barley firstfruits typified the translation of the 144,000.

In our last chapter, we represented the Son of Man descending on a cloud, sickle in hand to reap the earth. Now, the reaped grain is made into two finished loaves (Jewish and Gentile Christians) and presented to God. They stand on the "sea of glass." John records he saw this sea in his first vision of heaven (4:6), which then was empty but is now full of saints. *"Them that had gotten the victory over the beast, and over his image, and over his mark, and over the number of his name."* They had refused to worship Antichrist and the talking image. Also, they had refused to receive the mark in their forehead or hand. Having deciphered his name, they knew from its number he was the Antichrist.

This time the "sea of glass" is mingled with fire whereas before it was clear as crystal. Dr. Seiss says, "It is best taken as a sea of judgments which are poured forth in the seven last plagues, whilst in that regard at the same time a sea of blessed vindication and joy to those faithful ones whom the beast persecuted unto death." On the earth below, the angel who has "power over fire" (14:18) is executing the fiery indignation of God against all wickedness buy trampling the grapes in the winepress of God's wrath. It is as though these judgment-fires either were reflected upwards on the sea of glass, or else they were falling downward to the earth from that sea. At any rate, the saints are now above and beyond all this earthly activity while punishment is falling upon the wicked.

In chapter 12, God is shown as one who keeps His covenant by giving the seed of the Woman the power to bruise the Serpent's head. Hence, the scene begins with a view of *the ark of the testament,*" or covenant (11:19) wherein God's temple is opened to show the same. However, the word translated "temple" (*naos*) means the innermost chamber of it—the holy of holies in which the ark was placed. In the present chapter (15:5) the "temple," that is, this same innermost chamber again is opened to view the second time.

Now, it is called *the tabernacle of the testimony"* because the Ten Commandments at once represented a covenant and a testimony—a testament and a testimony. Did you ever think of the difference in the meaning of these two words? Wouldn't you rather someone give you something by his will and testament than by testimony against you? Hence, the ark in the holy of holies, which contained the Ten Commandments, was called both *the ark of the covenant* and *the ark of the testimony"* (Numbers 10:33, Exodus 25:22).

God will keep His covenant and translate His saints who are altogether obedient to Christ's warnings and ready for Him when He comes. That promise is the "great sign" of chapter 12 as well as the following chapters until the saints are seen on the glassy sea. *"Another sign in heaven, great and marvelous,"* brings God's *testimony* against the wicked into view. He condemns them to sore punishment. (Revelation 15)

His first and commandments are directed against idolatry, for these wicked people have been worshipers of Antichrist. Hear what He says: *"Thou shalt have no other gods before me. Thou shalt not make unto thee any graven image, or any likeness of anything that is in heaven above, or that is in the earth beneath, or that is in the water under the earth; Thou shalt not bow down thyself to them, nor serve them; for I the Lord thy God am a jealous God, visiting the iniquity of the fathers upon the children unto the third and fourth generation of them that hate Me."*

Again, God says: "Take heed unto yourselves, lest ye forget the covenant of the Lord your God, which He made with you, and make you a graven image, or the likeness of anything, *which the Lord thy God hath forbidden thee. For the Lord thy God is a consuming fire, even a jealous God. When thou shalt beget children, and children's children, and ye have remained long in the land, and shall corrupt yourselves, and make a graven image, or the likeness of anything, and shall do evil in the sight of the Lord thy God, to provoke Him to anger; I call heaven and earth to witness against you this day, that ye shall utterly perish from off the land whereunto ye go over Jordan to possess it; ye shall not prolong your days upon it, but shall utterly be destroyed.*" (Deuteronomy 4:23-26)

Thus, God severely condemns and threatens to punish idolatry. Certainly, those idolaters, worshippers of Antichrist, must be punished. God produces His testimony that indeed it shall be. The time has arrived for Him to *"destroy them which destroy the earth"* (11:18). His *"judgments on the wicked are made manifest"* by what follows.

CHAPTER XVI

The Vials of God's Wrath
(Revelation 15:6 – 16:6)

"Seven angels" in white linen robes, indicating spotless righteousness (19:8), with golden girdles are each given a vial *"full of the wrath of God"* against all unrighteousness, particularly against the detestable sin of idolatry. These angels come out of the very holy of holies. While they are punishing the wicked by emptying the vials of God's wrath upon them, *"the temple of God was filled with smoke from the glory of God and from His power; and no one was able to enter into the temple, till the seven plagues of the seven angels were fulfilled."*

These angels do their work very rapidly. The seventh trumpet blows for "days" when God is gathering together His elect *"from the four winds, from the uttermost part of the earth to the uttermost part of heaven"* (Mark 13:27). The "four winds" are mentioned in Revelation 7. This word "days" means a considerable length of time, for "day" does not always mean in the Bible precisely a period of twenty-four hours. Sometimes it is used as "time." The "day" of God's wrath means the *"time"* when His wrath is poured forth. Revelation 14:7 says, *"The hour of His judgment is come . . ."*

Again, *"Therefore shall her* (Babylon's) *plagues come in one day"* (18:8). These two expressions mean that the judgment and plagues of Babylon come rapidly and are of short duration. "In one day" may mean a literal day of twenty-four hours. Certainly, it means suddenly.

Punishment of wickedness may come about in two ways, either by being self-inflicted or God-inflicted. God once said to Israel, *"Hast thou not procured this unto thyself? . . . Thine own wickedness shall correct thee."* God may punish us, and He often does, by giving us our own way. In Romans 1, God gave wicked men a loose rein, who plunged into wicked unbelief, idolatry and sensuality. The Word says, *"The wrath of God is revealed against all ungodliness . . ."* How? In this manner: When men knew God, and did not glorify Him as God but fell into idolatry instead, then God *"gave them up"* to their own uncleanness (Romans 1:24), and *"gave them up"* to vile affections, (v. 26), and *"gave them up"* to a reprobate mind (v. 28). The end of giving men up to unrestrained wickedness is described at the end of this chapter in Romans as something awful to contemplate.

Paul, the apostle, tells us of a time coming when all restraint of wickedness shall be removed (2 Thessolonians 2:6-8). Afterwards, Antichrist will be revealed. The blowing of the seven trumpets means, I believe, the removal of the restraint the Spirit of God exercises over the conduct of evil men. When seven trumpets blow, seven great events, accompanied by others, follow:

(1) Hail, fire and blood destroy one-third of the grass and trees of that "fourth part of the earth" where the four judgment-agents—war, famine, pestilence and wild beasts rage. (8:7)

(2) One-third of the sea becomes blood. One-third of the ships and one-third of the fish are destroyed. (8:9)

(3) One-third of the fresh waters are poisoned, causing many deaths. (8:10)

(4) One-third of the sun, moon and stars are darkened, shining only part of their time each day. (8:12)

(5) A terrible locust-pest is let out of Hades, or "the bottomless pit," by a fallen angel. (9:11)

(6) A great war destroys 66,000,000 men.

(7) Satan comes to earth, in "great wrath," and raises up Antichrist and the False Prophet, who terribly persecute God's children. (16:13ff)

None of these occurrences, except the smiting of the sun, moon and stars as a sign of what is coming, is inflicted by God. Rather, these acts are the working out of the iniquity of war, of powers let loose from Hades, or of Satan himself. As described in the first chapter of Romans, these will come about because God gives men up to living out their own unrestrained evil passions as wrought by demons and Satan to which is added the direct work of fallen angels.

Now, we come to something entirely different in origin from the events under the seven trumpets, which we have been reviewing.[12] In our present chapter, holy angels come out of the holy Temple of God in heaven, and pour out His wrath upon the wicked. It is a punishment of unrestrained wickedness which God allowed men to work because they wished to. These punishments are:

(1) A painful sore upon the worshipers of the Beast who have his mark.

(2) A sea of dead blood which kills everything in it.

(3) Blood only in all the fresh water supplies as a punishment for the slaying of the martyrs.

(4) A scorching-hot sun.

(5) Darkness and awful, mysterious agony on the "seat" or throne of Antichrist—meaning terrible misery for all those about him.

(6) Next, the river Euphrates is dried up so that a great army headed by Oriental kings, may be able to cross it without delaying to make bridges.

We can imagine how they will say, when they arrive: "How fortunate! We wished to get to Jerusalem just as quickly as possible to help our great king (Antichrist) there, for he has called upon us to come to

---

12   See Appendix D.

his aid. We thought we would be detained here to build bridges, but the scorching hot weather has dried up the river. We can push forward without delay and arrive sooner than we expected."

And so, they rush forward to help sustain the infamous ruler, who is having troubles enough, under the vials of God's wrath. God allows them to hurry into the trap, which Palestine will prove to be to them. Christ is now about to come. After all His prepared saints have been translated from the earth, His coming will be so unexpected to those who do not believe the Bible that He says, *As a snare shall it come on all them that dwell on the face of the whole earth."*

These armies of the Oriental kings will never live to return home. At this time, *"three unclean spirits like frogs"* — out of the mouth of Satan; out of the mouth of Antichrist; and out of the mouth of the False Prophet—have gathered these Oriental kings and their armies together. *"The spirits of demons working miracles,"* they are called. Perhaps, it means demon-possessed human beings. Further on in the story, the kings respond to the call, doubtless with huge armies following them.

When we remind ourselves of what has already been said, we keep confusion away. The work of these seven angels with the vials of wrath represents in detail about the treading of the winepress in chapter 14. The order of events is: First, Christ reaps the earth of all the prepared saints. Second, an angel reaps the "vine of the earth" and casts the clusters (of the wicked) into the winepress. Third, the saints, resurrected or translated, are presented before God as the wheat-loaves of firstfruits. Fourth, the wicked are "reaped" and trampled in the winepress with the seven vials of God's wrath poured upon them.

The seventh is the battle of Armageddon when the blood mounts up to the horses' bridles.), and the great earthquake. Revelation 14:17-20 is expanded into chapter 16 where just before the battle of Armageddon, the voice of the Lord rings out an alarm: *"Behold, I come as a thief. Blessed is he that keepeth his garments, lest he walk naked, and they see his shame."* What does this scripture mean? All of God's prepared saints will have been translated before this time, but deluded Christians will still be on the earth—those whom Christ likened to five foolish virgins not sufficiently supplied with oil to enter with the rest into the marriage feast (Matt. 25:1-13). Although they have been shut out, the Lord still extends mercy to them. They need not be destroyed at Jerusalem since many are there when it is burned with fire at the time the awful earthquake comes. The White Horseman is still abroad saving souls. When this moment comes, if only these will remember the teaching of the Word, they can escape perishing with the wicked.

Very explicit directions are given to them in Zechariah 14:5. When this day comes, Jesus Christ will descend to the Mount of Olives. That mount will split in two, making a deep valley eastward from Jerusalem. They are instructed to flee at once from the doomed city through this valley and not rest until they reach a place called Azal. Although we do not know of such a place east of Jerusalem now, doubtless Christians at Jerusalem will know of such a place by the time these directions are to be followed.

After the Christians of Jerusalem are translated, then those left will realize they are in a dreadful predicament—left behind. God's awful wrath is about to break forth upon the city and the whole world. God never forsakes His own even though, like Jonah, they *"forsake their own mercy."* Having missed the best way, yet another way is provided. They are not outside God's mercy though they have failed to win a crown. Now, they have God's guidance on how to escape with their lives. Let us hope everyone will escape.

Notice the significant words, *"walk naked,"* which means going out on one's own feet. The translation has been missed. The same is taught by the Lord's cry over Babylon, *"Come out of her, My people, that ye be not partakers of her sins, and that ye receive not her plagues"* (18:4). In a later vision, John sees the destruction of Jerusalem under Antichrist—Babylon.

In his first epistle, John speaks of such Christians as being *"ashamed at His coming."* You will ask what is to become of such Christians? The answer anticipates the teaching of this book. However, it is that they will pass right through the Tribulation from first to last and exist with other mortals on the earth — to be ruled over by those who have won a crown, been made immortal, and who will reign with Christ on the earth a thousand years (20:4).

They will not have a part in the blessed first resurrection (20:6). Upon death, however, they will await the judgment of the Great White Throne (20:12) when the *"book of life"* will be again opened. If they are found faithful, they will be rewarded *"according to their works."*

A friend of mine, who lived in San Francisco, had the Lord to reveal that a terrible earthquake would soon wreck the city. She warned many to be ready for the calamity. Thinking her warning was all foolishness, even her own husband did not believe it. For many weeks before the earthquake, she wrapped her Bible inside her dress and other garments and placed them within easy reach. When the earthquake finally came, she was all ready for it and escaped with her clothes and her Bible. Others were not so well off by any means. They escaped naked and were very much ashamed until someone took pity and clothed them. I always think of this incident when I read this verse.

(7) The last plague is the destruction of Jerusalem and all the armies of the world which assembled there to defend Antichrist as the ruler of the entire world. Later, though, when the armies assemble to defend Jerusalem, they will change their minds by destroying and burning it with fire.

First, Jerusalem, and then the wicked armies around Jerusalem, will be destroyed in the battle of Armageddon (16:16). During this battle, the seventh angel pours out a vial of wrath upon Jerusalem in the midst of terrific thundering, lightning, rumbling sounds, and a terrible earthquake which breaks Jerusalem up into three parts. This earthquake will be the greatest one that has ever occurred in the history of the world. Cities all over the world will be wrecked by it, and islands will sink into the sea. Great mountains will explode, sending up into the sky huge stones that weigh as much as a hundred pounds. These stones will fall like hail upon the people, cattle, houses, and everything at hand and do terrific damage. It is recorded that even this destruction will not cause the wicked to repent but only to blaspheme the more.

CHAPTER XVII

"Babylon the Great"
(Revelation 16:17 to 17:8)

You wonder why I say some of these things happen at Jerusalem while the Bible says, *"Babylon."* Let me explain. We give places and persons names that are mere labels and do not describe the places and names at all. For instance, we perhaps name a baby boy, "Frank." As he grows up, he will be anything but frank. He may even be a little sneak and a liar. We will name a girl "Blanche," which means "white," when she is a Black girl. Or, we will name a town "Piedmont," meaning "foot of the mountain" when no mountain exists anywhere near it.

God never operates this way. Abram must be given a name suitable to the fact he was to be the father of all believers. God, therefore, changed his name to Abraham, which means "Father of a multitude." Sarai had a name which meant "princess," but it was not understood by the people because it was a foreign name. Therefore, God instructed Abraham to call her Sarah, which is Hebrew for "princess." King David's son was to be a "man of peace" so he was named Solomon, which means "peace." Jacob's name means "supplanter." He was always getting the advantage over others until one day he deeply repented. After a night of prayer when Jacob became changed in character, God named him "Israel," which means "prince of God."

You will recall many other instances to illustrate this point. See how Jesus changed the names of some of His followers when He chose them to be His disciples. He wanted them to have names that corresponded to what they were to become in character under His influence and through His redemption. He could not bear to have them going about with false names, so to speak, but with names that truthfully described them.

God is so true He will not make use of a false name. The word Jerusalem means "City of the God of Peace." Do you think, then, that the Bible, God's Word, would call that place when it is ruled by the terrible Antichrist, "the city of the God of peace?" I do not. God gives it another name. As long as it is ruled by Antichrist, He calls the place "Babylon," which means "the gate of the god." What god? Of course, the god is a mere idol, the talking image the False Prophet made. Christians will be killed who will not worship this god. Before Antichrist actually rules Babylon, it becomes so wicked that men rejoice and make merry over the dead bodies of the "Two Witnesses." God is also unwilling that the polluted place should be called "the city of the God of peace," so it is merely mentioned as *the great City which is spiritually called Sodom and Egypt, where also our Lord was crucified" (11:8)*

How very true god is in all His speech! The Bible says, *"Every word of God is tried."* Every word is put to the test to find out if it precisely describes the thing for which it stands. Let this teach us to be most careful in our speech, for the Lord has warned us: *"Every idle* [useless or false] *word that men shall speak, they shall give account thereof in the day of judgment."* We may well be sure that God's holy Book would not call that city, known in the Bible and by us by a name meaning "the city of the God of peace," by such an "idle" name as this, in His own day of judgment, when it is a scene of most terrible trouble and slaughter.

We cannot conceive of the greatness of this battle of Armageddon, and the frightful destruction which will follow when God pours out His wrath upon these armies, so that one and for ever all military power will be wiped off the earth: and then all the principal cities of the world will destroyed. Yet this will be a wonderful thing, for immediately after, Christ and His followers will set to work and restore everything in marvelous beauty and righteousness.

Of this great day of "the wrath of the Lamb," Dr. Seiss says: "The march of the terrific indignation of God on this occasion would, therefore, seem to be from the hills of Sinai, crashing through Idumaea (Edom), thundering by the walls of the holy city, and thence to the great fields of Esdraelon (Megiddo, the word from which Armageddon, meaning "hill of Megiddo," is derived), where the chief stress of the awful pressure falls." Yes the chief stress, when the Lord comes forth to battle, and the hosts are frightened away from Jerusalem by the terrible earthquake, which takes place. But the chief stress of the battle when the forces attack Jerusalem will be in the Kedron valley, at the southeastern corner outside the city wall, where the king's garden and winepress were, of old.

In Zechariah, 14th chapter, we learn more about this dreadful *"day of wrath"* or *"days of vengeance,"* as this time is called. It is said there, that when the armies shall surround Jerusalem, *"Then shall the Lord go forth, and fight against those nations, as when He fought in the day of battle." "His feet shall stand in that day upon the Mount of Olives, which is before Jerusalem on the east, and the Mount of Olives shall cleave in the midst thereof towards the east and towards the west, and there shall be a very great valley; and half of the mountain shall remove towards the north, and half of it towards the south."*

We have shown that all those who were "right with God" will have been caught up to heaven, before the great earthquake, when the Lord Himself comes forth to battle. But there will be Christians in Jerusalem and in Palestine at this time who have been all along more or less under the delusion of Antichrist until now. When the Christians who are ready are taken up suddenly to heaven, then these deluded ones will have their eyes opened. They will see how wrong they have been. And God, in His patience, has made a way of escape for even these, if only they will remember. They need not be caught in the dreadful trouble, if only, even at this late time, they will remember the instructions given them: *"Ye shall flee by the valley of My mountain* [R.V., that is by the valley created by the earthquake splitting Olivet in two]: *yea, ye shall flee, like as ye fled from before the earthquake in the days of Uzziah king of Judah, and the Lord my God shall come, and all the saints with Thee."*

Zechariah tells us more interesting things in this chapter: "All the land shall be turned as a plain from Geba to Rimmon south of Jerusalem: and it [Jerusalem] shall be lifted up, and inhabited I her place, ...from the tower of Hananell unto the king's winepresses." Here will be a great elevated plain, after the earthquake, nearly thirty miles long: and Ezekiel tells us that the Temple Platform (that is, the holy precincts immediately surrounding the temple), will, in the these days, occupy a space of about twenty miles square. This is to be the throne of our Lord Himself, when He comes with His saints to rule this earth.

Then John had two visions, in which he saw Babylon before its destruction again. One of the seven wrath-angels came and carried John away, in spirit, to see first a *spiritual* representation of this terrible "Babylon." He is taken into a wilderness (or desert), because through "Babylon" was in the very height of worldly prosperity (as the next chapter of the revelation shows), *spiritually* and morally it was utterly dead: all true religion was dead.

From the standpoint of heaven "Babylon" could only be represented as a horribly wicked woman, drunk with blood, for so many martyrs had been slaughtered in the city. "Mystery, *Babylon the Great, the mother of Harlots and Abominations of the Earth,*" was God's judgment of her character, branded on her forehead. This is not the name the city would give herself. The Authorized Version of the bible reads concerning John, *"When I saw her, I wondered with great admiration,"* but the Revised Version reads more correctly, *"I wondered with a great wonder"* or astonishment. John certainly did not admire "Babylon," but he was amazed to see how wicked it was. This wicked city was sitting on a scarlet colored beast who was *"full of names of blasphemy, having seven heads and ten horns."* This is now scarlet colored because of his many murders.

CHAPTER XVIII

MORE ABOUT BABYLON

(Rev. ch. 17:8 to 18:24)

Then in verses 8 to 18, the angel tells John some particulars about the city "Babylon" and Antichrist. John is not in a vision now; he is being instructed about the vision he has seen.

> (1) He is told, "the beast thou sawest was [alive on earth], and is not [is not now alive on earth]' and shall ascend out of the bottomless pit* (9:11, 11:7), and go into perdition" (v.8).

If the angel speaks these words of the time when John had these visions (about A.D. 96), then it seems as though the most ancient interpretation might be correct: that is, Antichrist might be Nero. He was the first Roman King to terribly persecute that Christians. He had been dead nearly thirty years; his name is Caesar Nero in Hebrew, number 666. The early Church were so filled with horror and dread of the monster that they constantly expected Satan to raise him from the dead; and why cannot this man, as easily as any other man, rise from the bottomless pit, when the time comes? But, Antichrist will never call himself Nero, when he comes back; he will only be recognized by his conduct and character; and Antichrist will not return as a mere Political ruler, but as a spiritual ruler as well, since he will pretend to be Christ.

> (2) Then as John was told how to recognize Antihrist by the number of his name, he is told how to know "Babylon" (v 9). *"The seven heads are seven mountains, on which the woman sitteth; and they are seven kings"* (R.V.).

If this "Babylon" is, as we think, Jerusalem under Antichrist, then we have an intimation that it is to be extended out over the Kedron Valley: the seven hills would be extended out over the Kedron Valley: the seven hills would be ion, Akra, Bezetha, Moriah, Olivet, Scopus, or perhaps Ophel, and the Mount of Evil Counsel. These hills have exited ever since Jerusalem came into existence, of course. We are told that they symbolize "seven kings" or kingdoms, and we take it that these kingdoms, like the hills, must belong to the entire history of J rusalem.

John is told (17:10) that five of these kingdoms had existed before John's day. *"One is"* [in existence] can mean nothing bet the Roman rule. Before John's day, and after Jerusalem was taken by David (1 Chronicles 2:4-8), the foreign kings who ruled over Jerusalem were 1st Babylonian; 2nd, Medo-Persian; 3rd, Greek, Alexander the Great; 4th Ptolemaic or Egyptian; 5th Selucid or Syriac. *"The other* [of the seven] *is not yet come.*" But it has since come; 7th the Mohammedan. Then it states: "*The beast* [Antichrist] *that was and is not, even he is the eighth, and is of the seven* [not "of the seventh," as some misread it] *and goeth into perdition.*" With Antichrist, the "wild beast" rule will end in perdition. The last "wild beast" will be called Babylon," as the first (Dan 7:8) was Babylon:; the last will be the final expression of all the seven before it; it will be "of the seven."

(3) Next, John is told (17:12) that ten kings or Kingdoms will have "*power as kings one hour with the beast.* These kings will only rule a very short time. They will form a confederacy with Antichrist, when he comes, and govern different parts of the world. These are those kings who will come and surround "Babylon," and fight, in the great battle of Armageddon. Those that come from the far east will find the Euphrates dried up (16:12). They and their soldiers under them will be summoned by the "*three unclean sprints*" (16:13). They will come (as stirred up by the infernal trinity, Satan, Antichrist and the False Prophet), to aid Antichrist in keeping his power against the coming Christ—the Lamb who with his 144,000 warrior-saints is descending to the earth (17:13,14).

(4) Then we are told that by this time "Babylon" is not only a city (Jerusalem under Antichrist), but also a world-side power (17:15, 18), "Babylon being the seat of the government.

(5) But no sooner do these kings reach Jerusalem, to fight for Antichrist and his world-wide rule, than something angers them, and they turn against the city, pillage it, taking all its treasurers ("*eat her flesh*"), and burn it with fire. God causes them to do this, for He wishes the city destroyed (17:16,17).

These are very plain particulars, are they not? We know what happened next: The frightful battle of Armageddon, and then the greatest earthquake that this world will ever see (16:18-21). We will speak more about this earthquake later.

We may be sure that such a mighty vision as John saw, when that great battle of Armageddon was shown him, and that terrible symbolic representation of the wickedness of "Babylon," must have set him thinking, thinking, thinking, until his head would be almost upset by it. We can fancy him saying to himself, over and over, "Will those poor deluded Christian, who will almost to the last imagine Antichrist is the real Christ (those who will not believe that Christ is really coming until after the translation of the saints), will thy really at last understand that Christ is coming to the earth as a 'snare' to the wicked, and as a '*thief in the night,*' to those not watching for Christ's return, and will they at any rate get out of the wicked, doomed 'Babylon' Christ talked of the '*sign*' of His coming. How will they be awakened at last?"

I think God gave John another vision to teach him about these questions that so perplexed him, and to tell him also how that wicked city which he had seen in symbol would appear to the worldly-minded people; how deceived they would be as to its true character. The Bible says, you know, *"That which is highly esteemed among men is abomination in the sight of God."* Chapter 17 told us of "Babylon" as an abomination in the sight of God: chapter 18 shows us the same wicked city as highly esteemed among men.

First as to the deluded Christians, and what would at last open their eyes, and cause them to flee from "Babylon"; Already we have been told, in the 14th chapter (v. 8) that the warning had been raised that "Babylon" was fallen—fallen very low in character, so that it was corrupting the whole world. It is said that *"an angel,"* or messenger, announced this. We must remember that the word "angel" means simply "messenger," and it is used of human beings in this book of the Bible. I do not myself think that anyone on earth saw an angel announcing that *"Babylon is fallen."* I think this means, as far as men will see and hear on earth, that many good people will begin at that time (stirred by the Spirit of God) to declare the true character of "Babylon," and to warn God's people as to it's true character. Still, some will not heed the warning, but will believe in Antichrist; even after all God's prepared people are translated.

John now (18:1) describes an Angel who approaches this earth, and He is so resplendent that the ground is lighted up with His glory. This description is so definite that, whatever we think of that 'angel" who first cried *"Babylon is fallen,* we must conclude that this is certainly some definite being, and who? This reminds us of that *"mighty Angel"* of chapter 10:1, with *"feet as pillars of fire";* this must again be the Lord Himself, for such language is never used of a human being, in the Bible. He declares, in plainest language, the fallen condition of "Babylon" *"Babylon the great is fallen, is fallen, and is become the habitation of demons, and the hold of every unclean spirit, and a cage of every unclean and hateful bird."* Then follows a further description of the corruption of the city, in the words of the Lord Jesus Himself. This is the voice of the Judge of the whole earth; He is declaring the wickedness of the city as a human judge might say: "I pronounce you guilty of murder," or "of arson," or of some other crime—and then follows the judge's sentence. So Christ's sentence follows here, but just before it is pronounced (for punishment will follow on the spot), all God's people, those deluded Christians remaining in it, are commanded to come away instantly, so that they may escape the same punishment. John ways: *"I heard another voice* [God's] *from heaven saying, Come out of her, my people, that ye be not partakers of her sins, and that ye receive not of her plagues."* The Christians now flee from the place, let us hope. Then follows the Judge's sentence: *"Reward her even as she regarded you and double unto her double according to her works: in the cup which she hath filled fill to her double. How much she hath glorified herself and lie deliciously to much torment and sorrow give her: for she hath said in her heart, I sit as a queen, and am no widow, and shall see no sorrow."*

The ten kings" must feel that they have been cruelly wronged by this city. They execute that sentence (17:16). But either they or other kings (but were there any other?), repent of what they have done, saying, *"Alas, alas, that great city Babylon, that mighty city! for in one hour will thy judgments come."* And merchants all over th world will lament over the destroyed city, for they were making money by trading with its very rich inhabitants; for Jerusalem will be very rich indeed under Antichrist. Listen, while we recount what they will trade in; gold, silver, precious stones, pearls, all kinds of cloth, ivory and all kinds of choice wood like cedar, and of vessels made out of them, and of brass, iron and marble, spices, wine, oil, flour and wheat, cattle of all kinds, choice fruits, horses and carriages, and *slaves.* This trade in slaves will be a special abomination in the sithe of God, we may be sure. And the ship companies, raders with foreign ports, importeres of foreign goods and wares of all kinds will also lament the destruction of "Babylon," for it will ruin them in business.

But God calls upon heaven, and all his holy apostles and prophets to rejoice for all the wickedness that has been destroyed fom foo the face of the earth by the burning of the city. *"And a might angel took up a great stone like a great millstone, and cast it into the sea, saying, Thus with violence shall that great city Babylon be thrown down, and shall be found not more a all."* And thus it will be suddenly finished, when, to add to all the rest, that terrific earthquake occurs. And there will never be another "Babylon" built on the site of Jerusalem. That city, and the civilization it supported, will be gone for ever, when all this destruction occurs. The very appearance of the country about Jerusalem will be totally changed. The old hills which have surrounded Jerusalem, all elevated plain, as we have seen the Temple or the Thorne of the King of kings and Lord of lords, Jesus Christ, who will come to rule, will, as we have shown, occupy a full mile of space, with an area around it of twenty miles square. So it may well be said that at this time "Babylon" will disappear for ever and nothing take its place, but the habitation of the Most High, and those who are appointed by Him to be close about his person.

And the word tells us why the city will thus disappear for ever: "In her was fond the blood of prophets, and of saints, and of all that were slain upon the earth."

This reminds one of what Jesus once said, when on earth, when He was warned not to enter Jerusalem, for fear Herod would kill Him. *"It cannot be that a prophet perish out of Jerusalem,:* for alas! Over and over has that city, in its history, persecuted and killed the very servants of God whom one would think that the city would have accepted even if other cities rejected them. This was so notorious that Christ, who never gave false witness nor exaggerated moral conditions, declared Jerusalem so full of murders of this sort, that upon the rulers of that city would come punishment for *"all the righteous blood shed upon this earth, from the blood of righteous Abel unto the blood of Zacharias, son of Barachias, whom ye slew between the temple and the altar"* (Matt. 23:35). And that punishment, at the first destruction of Jerusalem, was so terrible that over a million souls perished. But as the crimes will go on, more perishing at "Babylon" under Antichrist because they are prophets and saints, than at any previous time in history—millions must perish at its final destruction, and the city be wiped out once and for ever for its crimes. And the, with the complete purging of the region by fire, and the reformation of its very ground by an earthquake, there will arise on the same spot, an erection so magnificent that our wildest fancies cannot for a moment picture its grandeur and beauty.

PART VII

1. The Marriage of the Lamb.
2. A feast for birds of Prey Prepared.
3. Antichrist and the False Prophet sent to perdition.
4. Their soldiers slain whose bodies are devoured.
5. *"That old Serpent"* cast into the bottomless pit.
6. The saints Rule Earth for a Thousand years
7. Satan loosed, leads a Rebellion.
8. His armies Destroyed Fire from Heaven.
9. Satan sent to perdition.

CHAPTER XIX

Jehovah Shammah

The Prophet Ezekiel tells us some strange and wonderful things about the restoration of Jerusalem. Some of the things he tells are so difficult to understand that they are not believed, or are explained away as not *literal* prophecy, but symbols of something else.

We believe we must accept the prophecy as meaning precisely what it says, as far as we can understand it: and as for the rest, when we see it fulfilled we will understand it all.

He says that Jerusalem will one day be known be the name Jehovah-Shammah, or "Jehovah is there." Ezek. 48:35); and this seems to us to prove that it must be the one in which Jesus Christ sets up His rule on earth, when He comes again. After "Babylon" is destroyed, the ground being purified by the fire that burns it up, a new city and a new Temple will be built on the spot.

We are told in chapter 11 of an earthquake that clears the space for the Temple. Now we must consider another, and for more tremendous, earthquake (16:18-21), which divides "Babylon" (what is left after its burning) into three parts; an earthquake so terrible that it wrecks "the cities of the nation," how many we are not told. Islands sink into the sea: mountains are leveled to the ground, and a frightful volcanic eruption throws great rocks into the air, which fall down upon men, maiming, mangling, and killing them. Even this punishment does not cause them to fear God and repent—they only blaspheme.

It is impossible for us even to imagine he social disorder which will prevail, all over the world, when its great cities fall into ruin all at once, and that, just when the ten kings and their armies are fighting the great battle of Armageddon; and all military power, together with these kinds, will be destroyed.

We must think of Babylon, as Scripture calls it, not simply as a city, but as a capital of world-power. This world-power will together crash to the earth, never to rise again. Then, at that time—one of the most important of all periods in human history—the whole world will be prostrate under the King of Kings and Lord of Lords, who now comes visibly to rule. A description of this time is given in Zechariah, chapter 14: *"Then shall the Lord go forth, and fight against those nations* [assembled around Jerusalem]... *And His feet shall stand in that day upon the Mount of Olives, which is before Jerusalem on the east, and the Mount of Olives shall cleave in the midst thereof towards the east and towards the west and there shall be a very great valley; and half the Mountain shall remove towards the north, and half of it toward the south...All the land shall be turned into a plain from Geba to Rimmon south of Jerusalem; and it* [the city] *shall be lifted up, and inhabited in her place…And men shall dwell in it, and there shall be no more utter destruction; but Jerusalem shall be safely inhabited."*

Geba is north of Jerusalem a little way, and Rimmon is far to the south. The distance between the two places is thirty miles. All this hilly country will be leveled by the earthquake into a high plain, and towards the northern margin of it the Temple will stand, 1,000 feet square, with its outer enclosing wall, one mile long in each direction, a perfect square. The outside that square, the Temple precincts will be surrounded again by a square district between seven and eight miles long on each side (Ezek. 48:20), for the Priests and Levies.

Both Ezekiel and Zechariah tell us some wonderful things about Jerusalem restored. They both describe a great river which will flow out of Jerusalem, Ezekiel says from under the threshold of the East Gate, and Zechariah says it will divide into two prances of equal size: one branch will flow into the Dead Sea, east of Jerusalem, and the other into the Mediterranean west of Jerusalem.

The Jordan now flows through the land of Palestine from north to south; and there are t be these additional rivers running to the east and to the west. Ezekiel (ch47) in his vision, waded into this stream going eastward, unit it got so deep he had to swim; and when he got down to the Dead Sea he found it was no long (as it is today) so salty that no fish could live in it, but that the fishermen were spreading their nets to dry all along its western bank or fishing in its waters. And so it will be, sometime.

CHAPTER XX

"THE BRIDE, THE LAMB'S WIFE"
(Rev. Chapter 19 to 20:3)

A shout of praise is raised in heaven: "Hallelujah; Salvation, and glory, and honor and power, unto the Lord our God: For true and righteous are His judgments: for He hath judged the great harlot, which did corrupt the earth." But why is "Babylon" so persistently called a "harlot?" It is for this reason: The Lord made a very solemn covenant with the children of Israel, when He led hem out of Egypt into the land of Promise, Palestine. That covenant was that they should worship Him alone, not idols. The children of Israel, on their part, took this covenant upon themselves (it was not forced upon them). The covenant was so solemn that God speaks of it as of a marriage vow, and of the breaking of at vow and turning to idolatry as adultery. You will learn this by reading such passages as Deut. 4:23; 5:2-9, Jer. 2:2; 31:32; and Ezek. 16:1-8.

When the Israelites became settled in Palestine, Jerusalem was made the capital of their government, and according to Divine instructions, their religious headquarters, too. It is called a "harlot" by Isaiah (1:21): *"How is the faithful city become a harlot! I was full of judgment: righteousness lodged it; but now murderers."* This is the only city in the world, which God regards as His own. Hence, this is the only city, which, if unfaithful to God, could appropriately be called a harlot city. From this fact, we get its Scriptural title, *"Babylon, the mother o harlots."* Under Antichrist, with the place given over to his worship, God will not call it by a name meaning "city of the God of Peace" for He is a enmity against it. He calls it "Babylon" because as such it is a great international city, trampled under foot of many nations, as it is said (11:2), who talk many languages (10:11).

But Jerusalem, under the government of Christ, God will own.

Next, all the hosts of heaven joined in raise, saying, "Let us be glad and rejoice, and give honor to Him: for the marriage of the Lamb is come, and His wife has made herself ready: (19:7). By the marriage of the Lamb is meant the coming of Christ to live a Jerusalem.

The Lord once described this marriage of the Lamb in a parable. He did not represent this marriage quite the same as it was conducted in the days when He was on earth, nor as is customary with us today. In our day, the marriage feast is at the bride's house, and then the husband takes the bride away to the home he prepares for her. In the days when Christ uttered His parable, it was customary for the bridegroom to come, with the "friends of the bridegroom," and fetch the bride away to his own home, where there was feasting.

But the most ancient custom of all diffrs from both of these. You will find the ancient cusom described in Judges, chapter 14. Samson with his parents whent down to Timnath, where he was married at his bride's home, and the feast was in her home; and after the feast she did not leav home. In those early days, the bridegroom ordinarily made the bride's home his home, as did Jacob when he married Leah and Rachel.[13]

Here in the Lamb's marriage we have his ancient custom. It answers to God's marriage law: *"Therefore shall a man leave his father and his mother, and shall cleave unto his wife."* So here, the Lamb comes to live with the bride, Jerusalem, not to take her to His home, heaven. When Jesus uttered a parable to warn all to be ready for that marriage supper of the Lamb (Matt. 25:1-13), He represented those waiting at the b ride's home of Him to arrive; and as He approaches, they go forth to meet Him., and then return to the bride's home for the feast. Five of he virgins were not ready for His coming, and they were shut out. In Oriental countries, people make themselves so free in each others' homes that you must fasten u the doors, if you do not wish people to come in uninvited, to witness a wedding or join in feast.

In that parable, Christ is the Bridegroom, of course. The bride is Jerusalem restored, Jehovah-Shammah. The "friends of the bridegroom" come with Him to the feast. The five wise virgins are those who are prepared for His coming, and go out to meet Him, in that they are translated into His presence, as He approaches this earth. They are the *second* firstfruits. They do not stay up above, whither thy rose to meet Him, but they escort Him to this earth, and to Jerusalem, His bride. The foolish virgins, who were not ready to go out to meet Him, are not wicked people who go to hell. They believed in Him, and believed in His coming. The are left outside the marriage feast; they pass through the misery of the entire tribulation, lose the chance to reign with Him on the earth, and only appear again at the Great Judgment Day of God, described at chapter 20:11-15, at the end of the Millennium, when the *"book of life"* is again opened. They are saved, *"yet so as by fie"* the fire of the wrath of the Lamb. But this part we will consider later.

Next, verse 11, John sees the King of kings and Lord of lords, with all *"the armies of heaven"* in His train, coming to this earth for the final extermination of the wicked. He uttered a parable one, to illustrate this: *"A certain nobleman went into a far country to receive a kingdom for himself, and to return"* (Luke 19:12-27). This was frequently done, under the Roman Empire: A nobleman would go up to Rome, induce the Emperor to give him a crown, and come back and rule. But of Himself, Jesus did not say that He went in order to ask for it; it was given to Him; He went to *"receive it"* from the Father. He received that kingdom when He took that seven-sealed roll from the hand of the Almighty. (Rev. 5:7).

---

13   Abraham would not allow Isaac to go to live at Rebecca's home (Gen. 24:4,8), as his trusted servant thought might be required, because God had *expressly* called Abraham and Sarah its idolatry, (Joshua 24:3,3.)

The para le says that certain citizens of the country sent word after the nobleman, *"We will not have this man to reign over us."* So do wicked people, when they disobey Christ willfully, in the presence of the all-seeing Almighty. When the nobleman returned, he rewarded his faithful servants, according to their degree of efficient service in his absence. His reward was cities to rule over; to one he gave ten, to another five. So will Jesus Christ do when He returns to earth. He will give us cities and countries to govern, if we are faithful until He returns.

The twelve apostles will have places, of special honor. He said to them "Verily I say unto you that ye have followed Me, in the regeneration [when the earth is made over new], when the Son of man shall sit upon twelve thrones, judging the twelve tribes of Israel" (Matt. 19:28).

In the parable, before these faithful servants begin to rule, the nobleman commands: *"But those mine enemies, which would not that I should reign over upon white horses,"* which means, I think, borne on by the righteous upholding power of God; in fine linen, which is the righteousness of the saints. They have no part in the slaying of the wicked, which is done by the sharp sword of His mouth. He slays by the breath of His mouth. He only needs to speak the word and they are dead. John says:

"I saw heaven opened, and behold a white horse; and He that say upon him was called Faithful and True and in righteousness He doth judge and make war. His eyes were as a flame of fire, and on His head were many crowns:…And he hath on His vesture and on His thigh a name written, KING OF KINGS and LORD OF LORDS." Please read the whole description for yourselves, before going further.

We have no description given us of that marriage supper of the Lamb. *It is only spoken of, as we have shown; but now another sort of supper is called for.* It is a gruesome, horrid feast. This book of the *Revelation* is a strange book of couples and contrasts: We first see resurrected Old Testament saints (Jews) in heaven (4:4); and then a great body of resurrected Gentile saints (7:9). We first see a body of 144,000 Jews caught up to heaven (12:5); and then a body made up mostly of Gentile Christians who have been caught up (15:2). We read of *"the wrath of the Lamb"*; and then of Satan's *"great wrath."* We first see the ark of God's testament revealed in heaven; then the ark of His testimony. There are vials of prayers (5:8), and vials of wrath (chapter 15). We have a "great sign" of that covenant with woman's seed; then "a sign great and marvelous: of God's testimony against the wicked. The Two Witnesses do mighty signs, and punish those who oppose them with fire: then Satan gives power to the False Prophet, who *"doeth great wonders so that he maketh fire come down from heaven,"* and punishes all who will not worship Antichrist and his idols. Christ died and rose again from the dead. So Antichrist is someone who has been dead, whom Satan raises from the dead. Christ displayed His mortal spear-wounds t doubting Thomas; so Antichrist displays a mortal sword-wound to doubters. Jerusalem is rebuilt, and Antichrist rules there, God calls it "gate of a god, a harlot;

Jerusalem is rebuilt, and Christ rules there it is now called: city of the God of Peace,: the faithful bride of the Lamb; Jehovah-Shammah ("the Lord is there"). Next we come to the announcement of the marriage supper of the Lamb; then another supper a feasting of birds of prey upon dead bodies, is announced: *Come and gather yourselves together unto the supper of the great God,"* cries an angel standing in the sun, to unclean birds of prey: *"That ye may eat the flesh of kings, and the flesh of captains, and the flesh of mighty men, and the flesh of horses, and them that sit on them, and the flesh of all, free and bond, both small and great"* (20:17-18). This is how the great battlefield of Armageddon is to be cleaned up.

But even now, Antichrist, the False Prophet, and the kings rally their armies, badly as they have been cut up, for a final stand against Christ. How futile! They are seized alive—the Beast and the False Prophet—and hurled into the Lake of Fire, which means hell. All the rest are slain with the sword of His moth: a single word, and they are dead. Then Satan is taken and as the Lord has further use for him he is not yet put into the Lake of Fie but he is imprisoned in "the Bottomless Pit.:

But you will wish to know what is the difference between the Lake of Fire and the Bottomless Pit. Their relation to each other is like the relation of a common goal to a prison, or penitentiary. The Bottomless Pit is for temporary use; and the other for permanent confinement. The occupants of the bottomless Pit have not yet had, but are awaiting, their final sentence, which will be at God's Great Judgment Day. Those who go into the lake of Fire have been disposed of forever. We will learn a little more about this matter in chapter twenty-two of this book.

CHAPTER XXI

Our Wonderful Future
(Rev. Chapter 20:4-6)

Because I trusted and believed Jesus had forgiven my sins, I used to think that when I died I should go straight up into God's heaven, to remain there forever, singing His praises.

I did not get a great deal of comfort out of this belief, because we were told so little about our precise surroundings and occupations in heaven, that there was not enough to feed the imagination upon; and I could not have confidence in the mere air-castles of my own imaginings, knowing they might be far from the truth. Music was lovely, but to have *nothing* but harp music in heaven, however sweet those harps might be, did not seem sufficient. It would, indeed, be wonderful to see the Lord face to face, and to be forever free from sin. My thoughts could rest on these last two facts with *much* satisfaction.

But at another point I had little joy. Like Solomon in Ecclesiastes, sometimes I felt like saying of this world with its labour and sorrow: *"All is vanity and vexation of spirit.:* What was the use of so much hard toil to prepare for the duties of life, when there was the risk of dying soon, and all that had been learned would be *no use* in heaven, where the conditions of life were so entirely different?

And then, even if one did not die young, I noticed that the old people who had spent the longest time preparing, and who had had the most experience of life, were soon set aside by the younger generation, as of no use to them for early conditions rapidly change their complexion; and I must soon be set aside as too old for use, after all my preparation and experience. I was *not* lazy, but I liked to work *to purpose,* and there seemed such small purpose in life on earth, when one thought of its briefness. This made of life such a mystery.

But I was taught differently one day, and at once my life took on a new meaning. I saw a *use* for the labors of this life. I discovered a whole world in which I was yet to dwell, so like and yet so unlike this first earth-life; and where I could make further use of every scrap of knowledge and experience I gained. When I made that discovery, the meaning of life was no longer a mystery to me. Life became a very rich possession. I found I had been taught to read who passages of Scripture as though they were simply void of all sense, and this was the cause of my vacant views of the future.

We hall also reign with him" What does it mean? "The meek shall inherit the earth; and shall delight themselves in the abundance of peace." What does that mean? Have "the meek," as yet, inherited the earth? No! a war breaks out and the houses and lands of the people are appropriated at will by their own government, or by an invading enemy; and the government and invading enemy; and the land, not by their meekness, but by the very opposite—brute force. Those promises have never yet been fulfilled; and as sure as God's word is true, they must be fulfilled. When will the meek inherit the earth? After Christ has redeemed it out of the hand of Satan and of governments upheld by military power not before. When God redeems the land for us out of the hand of the terrible who have usurped it.

The Bible tells us, "The saints shall judge the world," 1 Cor. 6:2 and *If we suffer* [with Christ] *we shall also reign with Him* (2 Tim. 2:12). Daniel prophesies of the time when *"the saints…shall take the Kingdom"* and possess it forever; when judgment [the office of judges] is *given to the saints of the Most High,"* and *"the saints possess the Kingdom." "And the Kingdom and dominion, and the greatness of the people of the saints of the Most High (Dan.7:18, 22, 27)* and now we read in Rev. 20:4, *"I saw thrones, and they sat upon them and judgment was given unto them; and I saw the souls of them that had been beheaded for the witness of Jesus, and for the word of God, and which had not worshipped the beast, neither has image, neither had received his mark upon their foreheads, or in their hands; and they lied and reigned with Christ a thousand years."* What does *that* mean?

All these verses either *mean what they say*, or else the Bible is not true. When I stopped to think this over, and began to believe *just what the Bible says:* when I took as mine these plainly expressed promises of the Bible, then my thoughts found complete satisfaction in the contemplation, after death or translation, not only of sinless perfection in heaven, and the visible presence of my Savior, but in the rich imaginings of another (but sinless) earth-life of activity.

The Bible tells us that the very earliest of human beings lived to be nearly a thousand years old. Adam live 930 years; Seth 912, Enos, 905; Methuselah, 969; Lamech, 777; Noah, 950. After that the length of life began to decline. Two thousand years later than Adam, Shem lived only 600 years. Three hundred and fifty years later, Abraham live only 175years; Moses live only 120 years; and in our own day people live but about 70 years. The reason of this is that sin has brought about the gradual shortening of life. Sin produces disease, and disease is inherited from generation to generation, and so the mischief of sin and disease has increased through the centuries.

But Christ redeems us from Satan and sin, and then, if we are faithful to Him unto the end, He redeems the world for us. Then the government of this earth, redeemed from its "wild beast" (military) control, becomes the possession of *"The saints of the Most High,"* to be ruled by them for a thousand years. We are destined to be restored to all that would have been ours, had Adam never sinned, and had no one ever sinned since Adam's day and had life on this earth never been shortened. To be sure, we are destined to be restored to *more* than Adam lost; but *it certainly includes all that Adam lost.*

Formerly, I did not like the idea of Christ coming so suddenly—"as a snare upon the earth." It seemed to me unlike Him to suddenly come upon the unprepared Christians, and punish them if He found them unprepared. But now I understand the case so differently.

Let us get at the real idea. Human governments trust to war for their stability; and as time passes, forts are increased in numbers, guns and cannons are increased, and so are warships and soldiers. "Each nation tires to get the most of these things, so as to be the most powerful, the most stable of all the nations. But this is all done at variance to the will of Jesus Christ, the Prince of peace, not of war. And it is all, in the long urn, self-defeating and corrupting to the morals of the nations. We all know, too, how oppressive and cruel war is.

The Lord has made know His intentions, in this matter. When He can get a sufficient number of volunteer enlisted on His side (*not* armed with cruel weapons, however, but with the" fruit of the Spirit, love, joy, peace long-suffering gentleness, goodness, faithfulness meekness and temperance"). He intends to seize this earth for His own Kingdom and rule over it *visibly* Himself.

A General always seeks to get his soldiers into sympathy with himself, otherwise victory will be doubtful. He must have a powerful influence over their spirits. It is just so with Jesus Christ, our Commander-in-Chief. First of all, before he begins His conquest of the earth, He must have His soldiers, and they must be absolutely under His control, so that they will yield instant obedience to Him. Just think of it! He has spent nearly two thousand years mobilizing His troops! But the conquest of this world—and *such* a conquest!—is a very great thing. And while He could, with His almighty power, do it in a moment, yet if He conquered the earth by force and gave it back to us, when we were not His soldiers, or at the most were very indifferent soldiers, what would be the use? Satan would have it again, almost immediately.

No, when His forces are all mobilized, and are of a sufficient number for the conquest (there must be 144,000 Jewish men and then all the other Jewish men, women and children; lastly, there must be an immense Gentile Christian Army), then He will strike. Seeing ahead, as He does with His all-seeing eye, He knows of a time coming when all the kings of the earth will be assembled around Jerusalem—so He has let us into the secret, in this book, that when that moment arrives He will attack. "But," you say, "it's no secret. It's written in the Bible." Never mind; wicked people don't believe the Bible; they scoff at it as a book of fables; they do not read it so its *truth* is a secret, as far as *they* are concerned, all the same.

Now, he wars us, over and over again, to be ready for that moment. He says, repeatedly, *"Watch and pray,"* concerning this matter. *"Watch,"* He puts first, and that is what soldiers must do; the sentinel is a *most important* man in the army. *"And pray,"* for God to purify your life and enlighten our eyes, so that you can understand what is to come—see it when it is coming, and be all ready.

Then He says, "don't be frightened, when I come, because to accomplish my taks, I must come stealthily. I have prepared a snare for the enemy, but see to it that none of you get into it! Keep on your guard! Do not be frightened, for when I come, if in *your* lifetime, and if you are ready for it, I will suddenly catch you up, out of all danger, so be I on the watch."

You see, Satan—the Red Dragon—is really the commander-in-chief of the to her side, and he is far shrewder than any man—he will be shrewder than Antichrist and the False Prophet, when they come—and it is so necessary that he should have not time to scatter his forces that are collected about Jerusalem. Hence, *the precise time* of Christ's coming is kept a profound secret, to keep Satan from knowing it—for Satan believes the bible, if wicked men do not.

Satan hates Jerusalem above all cities in the world, because it is the city that God, from the very first, chose for His own. Satan has stirred up war after war against Jerusalem. It has been besieged and destroyed many times. He is *always* ready to collect armies o go up and fight around and against Jerusalem. But he will do so *just once too often*. He knows it already; and yet he goes against the city at every opportunity, always gambling (as it were) on the chance of escaping unhurt "this once more."

But at last the right moment will arrive. But only those at Jerusalem are likely even to suspect it, I think, For such immense wars must throw most of the world into confusing; all news will be censored; and those who live at a distance will not know precisely what is taking place at any given time. All at once, in a moment, Christ and the 144,000 will take up their position above Mount Zion. They will, of course, be invisible to the world. From that point Christ will call to Himself all the Christians of the world, dead or alive—the dead first.

After Christ rose from the dead, He had the same body he had before (John 20:20), but it was different. He could enter a room when the doors were carefully closed, apparently without opening them (John 20:19), and make Himself visible or invisible at will, and transfer Himself from place to place with wonderful ease, at last ascending up towards heaven until He passed beyond the clouds, out of sight (Acts1:9). It would seem that ordinary human bodies (and Christ possessed such a body, at first, from His mother), have been made dense and heavy by the decay going on in them, all the time; and it is this dense part which is cast off by us in death. It has precisely the form and general appearance of the *spiritual* body within; but it is really to be compared to the lobsters' shell when it is cast off. Now it is that *spiritual* body (yet the real, literal body of man, unencumbered of all its dead and waste material), which rises from the grave, in the resurrection of God's children (1 Cor. 15:44); and those who have not died, but are alive when Christ comes, will pass through a change in their bodies (1 Cor. 15:51,52) which will so lighten them up that they can rise from the earth *"to meet the Lord in the air."*

CHAPTER XXII

Our Service with the Lord
(Rev. Chapter 20:7-10)

That vast multitude of resurrected and translated saints in bodies, made *"like unto His glorious body"* after Christ rose from the dead, will return with Christ to rule this earth, the military power of nations having been all destroyed; all earthly kings deposed; Antichrist, the False Prophet and Satan put out of the way, and millions of wicked people taken off the earth.

According to prophecy, the Jews will settle in Palestine, and according to Christ's promise, the apostles will rule over them: *"Verily I say unto you,"* said Christ to His disciples, *"that ye which have followed Me, in the regeneration when the Son of man shall sit on the throne of His glory, ye also shall sit upon twelve thrones judging the twelve tribes of Israel"* (Matt. 19:28). Then we have seen how, by a parable, He taught the people, that those servants who made a profitable use of their opportunities while He was absent from this earth (gone away to a *"far country,"* heaven, *"to receive for Himself a kingdom"),* would upon His return, be rewarded, some with ten cities to rule, some with five cities to rule, etc. (Luke 19:12-27). Ma we be faithful, that we may reign with Him! The same thing is taught in the letter to the Church in Thyatira: *"He that overcometh, and keepth my works unto the end, to him will I give power over the nations; and he shall rule them with a rod of iron"* (Rev. 2:26-27).

But perhaps you ask who are to be ruled after this fashion? Why, think of the millions that will be left still on the earth, after the Tribulation is past; millions who either have not heard the Gospel call at all distinctly or if they did hear it did not choose to obey it, though they did not worship Antichrist, either! To be sure, the False Prophet threatened to kill all who did not worship Antichrist and his image or receive Antichrist's mark. And doubtless as many were killed as the False Prophet could lay hands upon, but he certainly could not compass the death of the hundreds of millions of inhabitants of the earth but (As we have said before, John's vision, in which he sees the False Prophet slaying the people, relates to Jerusalem and Palestine).

Therefore, everywhere, beginning with the apostles on their thrones at Jerusalem, the saints are scattered throughout the earth, each setting up a government over the territory assigned to them by the Lord. What a wonderful time of social reform this will be! These reigning saints will have bodies that never get tired; minds always alert; sprits never daunted; they never die—go right on with their work equally fresh each day, and all day long, setting the world to rights, beautifying the cities, parks and country fields. They have not Satan to contend against; no temptations to sin, and yet and yet they live among ordinary short-lived mortals who are sickly and sinful. Yet these mortals are not so malignantly sinful as formerly, when Satan went about tempting them and over-riding their wills. Now they are only weak and ignorant, and must be taught and governed the best qualities in the encouraged in every way possible, comforted, soothed and healed. Realizing the enormous powers of those who govern them, they will not attempt to resist. These are the days prophesied of by Isaiah (ch2) and Micah (ch. 4), when *"they shall break their swords into plowshares, and their spears into pruning hooks; nation shall not lift up sword against nation, neither shall they learn war anymore."*

The good work will go on from day to day, and from year to year, until finally sin will be almost abolished from the earth, and with the banishing of sin and healing of sickness, the lives of human beings will lengthen again gradually; intelligence will increase, and above all the *spiritual* life of the people will flourish. Covetousness will be known no more; neither will fraud, dishonesty and selfishness. Wealth will be evenly distributed, and a simple, innocent industrious life be chosen by all, instead of luxury, vice and indolence. Read this picture of those days which are coming: *"I create Jerusalem a rejoicing and her people a joy. And I will rejoice in Jerusalem, and joy in my people: and the voice of weeping shall be no more heard in her, nor the voice of crying. There shall be no more thence an infant of days, nor an old man that hath not filled his days: for the child shall die an hundred years old; but the sinner being an hundred years old shall be accursed."* (The though seems to be, no baby only a few days old shall die; no old man shall be cut off prematurely; at the age of a hundred, one will be still scarcely more than in his infancy; and should one be cut off by death as early as his hundredth year it would prove him a sinner whom God had visited with judgment.) *"And they shall build house and inhabit them; and they shall plan vineyards, and eat the fruit of them. They shall not build, and another inhabit; they shall not plant food and another eat; for as the days of a tree are the days of my people, and mine elect shall long enjoy the work of their hands. They shall not labor in vain, nor bring forth for trouble; for they are the seed of the blessed of the Lord, and their offspring with them. And it shall come to pass, that before they call, I will answer; and while they are yet speaking, I will hear. The wolf and the lamb shall feed together, and the lion shall eat straw like the bullock: and dust shall be the serpent's meat. They shall not hurt nor destroy in all my holy mountain."* (Isa. 65:18-25).

This describes Jerusalem, especially, but the same state of joy, peace and comfort will spread all over the earth, as the result of the rule of the saints, who will be taught by Jesus Himself, the King of the whole earth, how to rule the nations with perfect justice.

As you can see, this life is so like our present life that nearly all we have learned in this life can be put to good used during the Millennium, when we must teach the nations. The land, which is given them, they must be taught to cultivate. They must be shown how to build themselves comfortable dwellings, and be taught the ways and manners of a more civilized and cultured people than have ever yet inhabited this earth. Not one human being must be left ignorant, degraded, shiftless or neglected; all must be taught the highest possible state of development.

Whatever happens when the Lord thus takes this earth under control—I mean, if anyone should be unruly at first—all will be quickly subdued. The rule, though one of love and mildness, will be as firm as *adamant;* and no lawlessness be allowed. Soon perfect order, and that, without the exercise of any brute force will reign everywhere, and then great happiness and prosperity will follow. And after this has gone on for a thousand years, then the Lord will put human beings to the test. Not that He need to find out for Himself what is in many; He knows all thing. But man needs to know what is in himself, and God would have all know for themselves, by their own observation, that He is perfectly just.

This is His test, as described in chapter 20:7: "*When the thousand years are expired, Satan shall be loosed out of his prison,*" but only for "*a little season*" *(v. 3).* Now if, after this thorough drill in right living, any persons can be found who wish to sin, they must be removed from the earth altogether—sent to Hades to await the Great Judgment Day.

And John proceeds to tell us that such rebels will be found—people who have only done ight because they did not dare to do wrong, but who in their hearts still loved unrighteousness. Satan easily makes these people his dupes, by telling them to follow him and they an readily conquer Jerusalem and seize the kingdom and rule the earth as they please. Strange to say Satan gets an immense following of people, called Gog and Magog, band they arch up to Jerusalem and besiege it, but God rains down fire from heaven and kills them. Satan is seized, and this time he is thrust into hell (Gehenna), "*the lake of fire and brimstone, where the beast and the false prophet are,: and where the "shall be tormented day and night for ever and ever*" *(20:7-10).* This is the end of Satan, as far as human beings on earth shall ever know.

Now I am wondering if any of the children who hear this story of Jerusalem and the whole world, when governed by the Lord Jesus Himself, are saying "But she has not told us one thing about the children who live during the Millennium." They cannot be governing cities and countries, putting drink shops out of existence, and teaching people how to be good. What will the children be doing? "When all the grownups are so useful and holy, will it no be rather hard for us children to keep from doing something to displease them? Will we not have to be so awfully, awfully good, that we cannot have any good times at all?"

Why, that's just the good part I'm coming to! Grown-ups will not come home tired from their work; and will not always be in a hurry, and cannot be bothered; and will not have headaches, and be worried with many cares. They will have time to spend with the young folks, having a good time with them. Why, the bible tells us what a good time the children, too, are going to have. Just listen to this: "*I am returned unto Zion, and will dwell in the midst of Jerusalem: and Jerusalem shall be called a city of truth: and the mountain of the Lord of hosts the holy mountain. Thus saith the Lord of hosts; There shall yet old men and old women dwell in the streets of Jerusalem, and every one* [of these old people] *with his staff in his hand for very age. And the streets of the city shall be full of boys and girls playing in the streets thereof*" (Zech. 8:3-5).

That looks as though the old folks loved to have the girls and boys playing all about them, does it not? And just as it is at Jerusalem, we may be sure it will be in every other city. No fear of bad boys and rough company; nor of motors and officious policemen, drunken men, and all the rest. Just a good time out on the public street, where most children love best of all to play; only while the world is so wicked, and the streets unsafe, careful parents cannot allow it.

CHAPTER XXIII

When Will He Come?

The Lord would gladly have come along ago and He has been ready to come all the time. But when He comes, it must be that He will exterminate the wicked from the earth, so as to give the good all possible chance; and He is waiting, all the time, to gather in as large a number of the good as possible. Say for instance, that he waited twenty years for your grandfather to make up his mind to turn from sin to righteousness, so that He need not send your grandfather to the fate of the wicked; and in the meantime your father was born, and He waited for fifteen years to get him saved before He came ; and now He sill waits for your conversion before coming. Then multiply your grandfather's case, and your father's and you own by thousands more, quite similar, all over the world—unconverted people whose friends have prayed for their salvation, and the Lord wishes to answer those prayers, and not cut them off in unrighteousness. Can you not see how rapidly the centuries would roll round, as the Lord waited in His longsuffering, and yet, all the time, He himself be ready to come? This is Justas Peter represents:

> *"There shall come in the last days scoffers, walking after their own lusts, and saying. Where is the promise of His coming? For since the fathers fell asleep, all things continue as they were from the beginning of the creation."*

Yes, even now already they are blasphemously saying, "That promise in the Bible that the Lord would come is proved false, because He has not come; two thousand years, almost, have passed away, and things remain just as ever. Here is your proof that the Bible is false."

And all this time the Lord's coming has been very near, and we have been keeping it back by our delay to get ready. Let us not mock because He has not come; let us be thankful that, in His longsuffering, He has been willing to wait.

In 1890, a great Students' Missionary Conference was held in London, and a large chart of a problem in arithmetic was hung up before the people. That arithmetic was hung up before the people. That chart was a demonstration, in figures, of the question:

If there were only ONE Christian in the world, and he worked a year and won a soul for Christ; and IF these two continued each year to win another should for Christ; and IF everyone thus won to Christ led into the kingdom one soul each year; in how many years would the world be won to Christ?"

Had I worked that problem out all by myself, I should never have believed that the real answer was the right one, for it was so surprising. But students, just out of the University, had worked the problem out; and there was the complete demonstration, so that the correctness could be tested, and no one was able to confute the answer. That answer was this; IN THIRTY-ONE YEARS.

Now we need not split hairs by arguing that every one converted to Christ would not live thirty-one years there after, and be able to save on should each year. The statement is quite sufficient to prove to us what we wish to know, namely, why Christ could, in all truth, hold out the possibility of His speedy return, and why St. Paul and all the other apostles could and why St. Paul and all the other apostles could and why St. Paul and all the other apostles could stir the Christians up to that hope constantly. It was not God's will that Christ's return should have been so long delayed, but we are left with freedom of choice, and we have delayed Christ's return. God has not seen fit to say much about the dead—the good dead—shall spend their time while waiting for good dead—shall spend their time while waiting for Christ's return. They will be in paradise: at one after death, as Christ promised the dying penitent thief on the cross; or in "Abram's bosom," as He shows us the good Lazarus was after death; the latter expression means that same paradise. It was used by the Jews to signify the place for the good dead. They will be conscious, and "in bliss, with Christ" as St. Paul says, and waiting to come with Christ to rule this earth.

St. Paul tells us that we are to comfort those who are in bereavement in a very different way than that of putting before them a mere prospect of reunion after death. He says, *"Comfort one another with these words:' The Lord Himself will descend from heaven with a shout, with the voice of the archangel, and with the trump of God; and the dead in Christ shall rise first; Then we which are alive and remain* [on earth] *shall be caught up together with them in the clouds, to meet the Lord in the air; and so shall we ever be with the Lord.'"* And will we remain up in the air? No, not at all. We have already seen that this being caught up to meet the Lord in the air means that, like the wise virgins of the parable, we merely go out to meet the Lord, and bring Him down to the earth to remain here with us. This is the hope—a hope of a crown and service on earth, not merely of rest in heaven—which the Bible sets before us; and a hope of which Paul says in this same Chapter (1 Thess 4:13), *"I would not have you ignorant concerning them that are asleep, that ye you ignorant concerning them that are asleep, that ye sorrow not, as others that have no hope. For if we believe that Christ died and rose again, even so them also* [our loved ones] *which sleep in Jesus will God bring with Him."* And it has always been within the possibilities for Christians by their spiritual zeal, to have brought all their loved ones who died in Christ back to them again, alive, and within a generation or two. All that was needed was for all Christians to *get things ready* for the coming of the Lord, without any delay, to *"seek first the kingdom of God and His righteousness."*

Therefore, when our loved one dies, we should not, like doubting Thomas, say, *"Let us also go that we may die with him:* (John 11:16). Pathetic, doubtful comfort that! Every death of a loved one should stir our hearts, *not* with a desire to die, too, but with an intense, holy (not rebellious) ambition not to see another loved one die, and not to die ourselves, if only by our faithfulness and diligent service for the salvation of others, we can bring the Lord to this earth in our own day. We should rather look to His coming bringing our loved ones' return with the Lord to this earth again. This should be the Christian's hope and high ambition.

CHAPTER XXIV

The Final Great Judgment Day
(Rev. ch 20:10-15)

A full thousand years have now passed since the saints came to earth to rule it. Jerusalem has been besieged unsuccessfully by Gog and Magog and Satan banished for the earth into eternal punishment with Antichrist and the False Prophet. All during this period of a thousand years the ordinary mortals have been dying in the usual way on earth, but with an increasing length of days, few if any being cut short in years.

After God and Magog with Satan have been conquered, and not a human being left on earth who wishes to sin, or who will sin, then the reign of the saints on earth is over—there is no one there who needs to be governed; no one to whom to teach righteousness "And they shall teach no more every man his neighbor, and every man his brother, saying, know the Lord; for they shall all know me from the least to the greatest of them" because, as Isaiah and Habakkuk say, *"the earth shall be full of the knowledge of the Lord, as the waters cover the sea"* (Isa. 11:9; Hab. 2:14)

St. Paul tells us that next after this Jesus Christ Himself gives over the government to God, the Father. Christ "must reign till He hath put all enemies under His feet," and "when He shall have put down all rule and all authority aone'nd power," "then cometh the end when He shall deliver up [R.V.] the kingdom to God, even the Father" (1 Cor. 15:24,25, transposed).

We come now to a scene following upon the delivering over of the Kingdom to the Father. John says: I saw a great white throne, and Him that sat on it, from whose face the earth and the heaven fled away; and there was no place for them." Who is this? God and Christ as one' Christ as more that the King of the kings of this earth, in full possession of His Godhead: Onc with God the Father, whose the Kingdom now is. He is about to judge the world for the last time, to judge three classes of beings. 1st, Those persons who though Christians, because of their unpreparedness (like the foolish virgins who did not provide sufficient oil with their lamps) were left in the "outer darkness" When the Bridegroom came. They were not translated with the saints, but were killed perhaps during the great battle of Armageddon, or lived throughout the great Tribulation and into the Millennial age, dying like ordinary mortals; not given crowns and dominions nor lengthened days. 2nd, Those mortals who have been born and died during the Millennium. The test will not be, as with us, whether we believed in and trust the Lord Jesus, because the Lord Jesus will be ruling visibly over the earth throughout the Millennial age, and all will believe in Him, but some (the rebels of Gog and Magog) will, like the demons, "believe and tremble" (James 2:19), but not yield their hearts wholly to Him. These dead will be judged" according to their works" (v.12). 3rd, To judge all the wicked who, since the beginning of the world, have died, and have been in Hades all this time, for none of these has any part in the first resurrection (v 5).

At the time of this great judgment day, the earth will be enveloped in flames. St Peter describes this time: "*The heavens shall pass away with a great noise, and the elements* [all solid parts] *shall melt with fervent heat, the earth also and the works that are therein shall be burned up. Seeing then that all these things shall be dissolved, what manner of persons ought ye to be in all holy conversation and godliness, looking for and hasting unto the coming* [rather "hastening the coming"] *of the day of God, wherein the heavens being on fire shall be dissolved, and the elements shall melt with fervent heat? Nevertheless we, according to His promise, look for new heavens and a new earth, wherein dwelleth righteousness*" (2 Pet. 3:10:13).

This day comes "*as a thief in the night,*" too for this time not even a trumpet is sounded to warn the faithful of its coming. And besides, there is nothing for the faithful to fear or to flee from—no Antichrist; no great battle of Armageddon to catch the unprepared. Those who pass through this last judgment will be mostly evil persons whose names are "*not found written in the book of life*" (v. 15). *Those who have lived and reigned with Christ a thousand years*" have passed their judgment day a thousand years before. They will not be hurt in the least by this fire which dissolves all things. The pious mortals who have died during the Millennium will now be raised to life, and rewarded "*according to their works*"(v. 12). Lastly. since the "book of life" is produced again as "the Lamb's book of life" (20:.12, 13:8, and 21:27), we must believe that some, who would have been translated at the Seventh Trumpet had they been ready, forfeited the blessedness of the exaltation and service of reigning with Christ on the earth a thousand years. In the end, they are acquitted at the Great Judgment Day because their names are found in "the book of life." They are saved, "yet so as by fire," being acquitted at the Great Judgment Day.

The burning of the earth and the atmosphere about it is what Peter meant when he says, "the heavens being on fire" (II. Peter 2:12). Also, we read, "the heavens fled away," and all melts with the "fervent heat." Such action secures the destruction of every corrupting thing, and the whole is purified through and through. All that can die is destroyed by the fire. The very abode of the wicked dead, which seems to be somewhere in the bowels of the earth in Hades, is burnt out and cleansed by fire. "From this period on, no need will exist for a place for the dead (Hades), awaiting their final punishment, for there will be no death. Both death and Hades are cast into the "lake of fire," into which the Antichrist, the False Prophet, and Satan are cast "along with "*whosoever was not found written in the book of life . . .*" in this second death (v. 14, 15).

CHAPTER XXV

"A New Heaven and a New Earth"
(Revelation 21:1 – 22:7)

Two words mean "new" in the Greek language, whereas the English has only one. *Neos* means "new" in the sense of "recent" or just beginning. *Kainos* means "new" in the sense of character or condition without special reference to age. *Kainos* is the word John uses when he says, *"I saw a new heaven and a new earth."* He means he saw the earth and its surrounding atmosphere made new again by having passed through the fire. A manufacturer of jewels can take a lot of old gold and make a new gold ring out of it. Likewise, the earth will one day be put through a melting, refining, remodeling process. Out of it, a "new earth" will come such as John saw.

First, John mentions about the new earth, *"there was no more sea,"* which one would expect. The intense heat has evaporated the stagnant, salty sea entirely. From henceforth, only fresh water will be found on the earth. Also, the space the sea occupied will now be needed for the habitation of all the good people who have lived throughout the ages — millions upon millions of them.

Then, the new Jerusalem for God's people does not at all correspond to the description of the Jerusalem of the Millennial age. For instance, no temple is in it (v. 22), and the Temple was the *great thing* in the Millennial Jerusalem. *"And the city had no need of the sun, neither of the moon to shine in it; for the glory of God did lighten it, and the Lamb is the light thereof."* This phenomenon is not because the sun and moon are blotted out of existence, but because the light from God and Christ's own person is so much more brilliant than light from material bodies like the sun and moon. Since the Divine presence is always in New Jerusalem, *"The nations of them which are saved shall walk in the light of it;"* and the saints who reign with Christ, and *"the kings of the earth, do bring glory and honor unto it"* (v. 24).

And, we may be sure "there shall in no wise enter into it anything that defileth, neither worketh abomination, or maketh a lie; but they which are written in the Lamb's book of life" (v. 27). And oh! how happy all will be! "God shall wipe away all tears from their eyes; and there shall be no more death, neither sorrow, nor crying, neither shall there be any more pain; for the former things are passed away" (v. 4).

Why does John say this "New Jerusalem" was coming *"down from God out of heaven?"* The city this time, unlike the Millennial Jerusalem, seems to be of a heavenly nature. Surely its costly materials were never found on earth. Were not the earth to be made over and the seas abolished, no room for such a city would exist that is 1,500 miles in length and in breadth. Says Dr. Seiss: "The base of it would stretch from farthest Maine to furthest Florida and from the shore of the Atlantic to Colorado. It would cover all Britain, Ireland, France, Spain, Italy, Germany, Austria, Prussia, European Turkey and half of European Russia taken together!"

Strange to say, it is as high as it is long and wide — 1,500 miles high! By the time this city comes into existence, human beings will have taken on wonderful new powers, so that moving upwards and downwards will be as easy and natural as moving to and fro. The city is spoken of as *"Having the glory of God; and her light* (which streamed from "the Lord God Almighty and the Lamb") *was like unto a stone most precious, even like a jasper stone, clear as crystal"* (v. 11). A *jasper stone "clear as crystal"* does not appear to be an ordinary jasper but a diamond. The light will shine with radiancy and many colors like a diamond, only infinitely more brilliant.

"The foundations of the wall of the city were garnished with all manner of precious stones." Their colors are probably: 1. diamond; 2. blue; 3. bluish grey; 4. grass-green; 5. carnelian striped with green; 6, cornelian striped with brown; 7. golden; 8. sea-green; 9. yellow; 10. translucent pale green; 11. red; 12. violet-blue. Each of these twelve enormous precious stones has the name of an apostle engraved on it. With all these various and brilliant colors, most nearly transparent as well, one can understand how the general effect was to John like one great diamond, as he describes it in verse 18: *"And the building of the wall of it was of jasper."*

Although each one of the twelve gates was made of "one pearl" of enormous size, these gates always stood open (vv. 21, 25). The city was of pure transparent gold. Although no temple was in the city, "the throne of God and the Lamb" (22:1) and a pure river of water of life, clear as crystal" came out from under the throne. It is quite beyond us to comprehend all this description fully. As John saw it, the city was *"descending out of heaven from God."*

Since it had not yet touched the earth, this river and *"tree of life which bare twelve manner of fruits"* are all heavenly, not earthly. We shall only fully understand these things when they come to pass or when we enter this New Jerusalem. It is written, *"The leaves of the trees were for the healing of the nations."* Even today, we have the healing power in the water of life and in the leaves of the tree of life in our salvation through Jesus Christ.

Canon Payne Smith says: "As the Bible begins, so does it end with that tree of life. Its meaning in the last chapter of the book of Revelation is no longer veiled as *'the pure river of the water of life'* is the grace of the Holy Spirit, and the *'tree of life'* is *'the living bread which came down from heaven, of which if anyone eat he shall live for ever'"* (John 6:51).

Someone seems to have spoken to John just then. He said, "There shall be no more curse; but the throne of God and of the Lamb shall be in it; and His servants shall serve Him. And they shall see His face; and

His name shall be in their foreheads. And there shall be no night there; and they need no candle, neither light of the sun; for the Lord God giveth them light; and they shall reign (not merely a thousand years but) for ever and ever."

I suppose John was so staggered and overwhelmed by this wonderful vision of New Jerusalem that he could not realize it at all. Perhaps he even thought: "Is this vision of something *real*, or am I dreaming?" For the voice continued: "*These sayings are faithful (believable) and true; and the Lord God of the holy prophets sent His angel to show unto His servants the things which must shortly come to pass.*" I wonder if John began now to recognize the familiar voice: "*Behold, I come quickly; blessed is he that keepeth the sayings of the prophecy of this book.*"

The visions are now over. John has seen the last one, and he has heard the voice of his Master confirming them all as an actual representation of things which will really come to pass and be known to God's servants by actual experience in due time. See the *special pains* taken to teach us the importance of studying, pondering and trying to understand this book. At the very beginning (1:3) it is said; "*Blessed is he that readeth, and they that hear the words of this prophecy, and keep* (treasure up) *those things which are written therein.*" At the end of the visions, the blessing is repeated on him "*that keepeth the sayings of the prophecy of this book.*"

CHAPTER XXVI

"The Spirit and the Bride Say Come"
(Revelation 22:8-21)

It was *"one of the seven angels that had the seven vials"* full of God's wrath who took John to see *"Babylon the Great,"* first in its state of spiritual degradation, and then in its state of worldly grandeur. John also was shown Jerusalem Shammah, the New Jerusalem of the Millennial age. The truth of the visions John saw—no mere imaginings—was impressed upon him when angel said, *"Blessed are they which are called unto the marriage supper of the Lamb... These are the true sayings of God"* (19:9).

At the angel's voice, John fell at his feet to worship him (19:10). However, the angel said: "See thou do it not; for I am thy fellow-servant, and of thy brethren that have the testimony of Jesus; worship God; for the testimony of Jesus is the spirit of prophecy." This voice belonged to some prophet who had become an angel in heaven. Again, "one of the seven angels which had the seven vials" took John to see the "holy Jerusalem, descending out of heaven from God" (21: 9, 10). John says: "When I had heard and seen, I fell down to worship before the feet of the angel which shewed me these things."

This angel must have been a second wrath angel, for it is not likely that John would attempt to worship the same one who had reproved him before. The angel said, *"I am thy fellow servant and of thy brethren the prophets."* In his vision, John sees two great angels with the tremendous authority to execute God's dread judgments on the earth. Yet, they were once human beings on earth that were prophets of God. These men, however, possessed human faults and frailties but were forgiven, cleansed by the precious blood of Jesus, raised to heaven, and exalted to fulfill God's highest offices. What a wonderful prospect unfolds of blessed exaltation and usefulness if we remain faithful!

Even though so highly exalted, how humble these angels are! How little they care for mere, outward conditions as compared with character! At this moment, John was probably a poor, despised, exiled slave in the mines of Patmos. Yet, these glorious, great angels will have no kneeling to them such as the pettiest kings on earth require of their subjects.

The angel charged John: *"Seal not the sayings of the prophecy of this book."* Then, it ought to be an easy matter for us to understand most of the book. The book is not difficult to understand if only first *believed to be literal truth.* Men first reject the plain teaching that Christ is to come a second time to this earth to redeem it and then settle redeemed men on the earth as His co-laborers to rule it and subdue its lawlessness. Having refused to believe this elementary truth of the Word, they begin to *explain away* rather than to *explain* this book. When we accept the book as *meaning what it says,* it can be understood without much difficulty.

The records of this book as Dr. Seiss says: "Constitute His last and crowning legacy to his Church and people. They are written by His appointment and command. They are put into our hands by the specific direction of eternal power and Godhead. They are therefore God's word to us. And if He commanded the writing of them, I cannot see how men are to excuse themselves from the reading and study of them; or how any Christian can think lightly of them, or put them from him as of no practical worth, and yet retain his holy faithfulness to the plain will and inculcations of our blessed Lord and Judge."

Paul, the apostle, tells us: "The mystery of iniquity doth already work; only there is one that restraineth now, until He be taken out of the way. And then shall be revealed the lawless one (Antichrist), whom the Lord Jesus shall slay with the breath of His mouth" (R.V.). That restraining power is the Holy Spirit. He softens the heart, and convicts of sin, leading to repentance and forgiveness. We make a great mistake when we imagine we shall always be able to repent if we wish. The mistake is that we may come to a time when, though we know it is the wisest, most important thing to do, when we will be involved in most awful misery if we do not. However, if we do not, we cannot merely wish to repent. As surely as God's forgiveness is a gift, so surely is the power to repent a gift.

God "opened the door of faith unto the Gentiles" (Acts 14:27), and that "God also to the Gentiles granted repentance" (Acts 11:18). While Paul, whose message would not be received by the Jews at Rome, declares the word of Isaiah applies: "Hearing ye shall hear, and shall not understand; and seeing ye shall see, and not perceive." (Acts 28:26).

Elsewhere he tells us the Jews were hardened at this time because they rejected Jesus Christ. They were hardened in that God did not soften their hearts, and they did not feel like repenting. God promises before the Lord comes, the hearts of the Jews will be softened again, and they will repent in great numbers. For instance, Zechariah says: "And it shall come to pass in that day, that I will seek to destroy all the nations that come against Jerusalem. And I will pour upon the house of David, and upon the inhabitants of Jerusalem, the spirit of grace and supplications; and they shall look upon Me whom they have pierced, and they shall mourn for Him, as one mourneth for his only son, and shall be in bitterness for Him, as one that is in bitterness for his firstborn" (Zechariah 12:9-10). Therefore, repentance for sins is the gift of God similar to the forgiveness of sins.

Now, we come to a time when a most awful fate will be pronounced upon sinners when Christ comes in judgment: "He that is unrighteous, let him do unrighteousness still: (R.V.) "he that is filthy, let him be filthy still" (v.11). The door of repentance is closed forever with the Lord, free from all temptation. Their fate—most happy fate—is fixed too, forever. "He that is righteous, let him be righteous still; and he that is holy, let him be holy still." A fixed fate for the unrighteous and filthy and a fixed fate for the righteous and holy is the reward which each one receives from

Christ, *"every man according as his work is"* (R.V., v. 12) when the Lord comes in swift judgment.

Those who *"do His commandments"* shall have a right to the tree of life, whose leaves are for the healing of the nations, and they *"may enter in through the gates into the city"* —New Jerusalem. Outside that celestial city far beyond reach of the mercy of God will be those who have sinned so long and deeply they will not care to repent." These *dogs* (men given over to unclean, ravenous appetites) *sorcerers, fornicators, murderers, idolators, liars"* will have their part in the lake of fire (20:15).

The wonderful book of the Revelation draws to its close with the Lord knowing that its study would be neglected by Christians and its value and authority discounted just as has been the case. In His faithful care for His thoughtless, foolish followers, He adds His most solemn seal to all that John has written. No one shall ever say, "John was mistaken or mad when he wrote all these wild fancies! We believe John's Gospel and his epistles, but the Revelation proves John's mind became unsettled through his hardships as an exiled slave!" No, no one shall ever have one excuse for trying to weaken the authority of this last book of the Bible!

Jesus Christ Himself seems to take the pen in hand now: "I, Jesus," He writes, "have sent mine angel to testify unto you these things in the churches. I am the root and the offspring of David, and the bright and morning star." It is as though He said, "All of you understand now that you don't have to account to John for disbelieving this book or for treating it lightly. John has written it as My secretary at My dictation with the aid of the angel whom I sent to instruct John. Let anyone neglect, slight, mutilate or add to this book, and he must settle his account with me, Jesus Christ, in a day of reckoning."

What stronger proof could He give of His identity as the very Son of God, *"the root and offspring of David, and the bright and morning star,"* than in the very midst of this stern language, He interrupts it by one more yearning invitation for us to come and be enclosed in His arms of love forever: *"The Spirit and the bride* (the beautiful New Jerusalem) *say, Come. And let him that heareth say, Come. And let him that is athirst come. And whosoever will, let him take the water of life freely."*

One is reminded of His outburst over the wicked, violent Jerusalem that crucified Him in the midst of most fearful denunciations and warnings when he cries, *"O, Jerusalem, Jerusalem, thou that killest the prophets, and stonest them which are sent unto thee, how often would I have gathered thy children together, even as a hen gathereth her chickens under her wings, and ye would not!"*

If any are left outside new Jerusalem, it will not be for lack of a warm invitation to enter. It will only be because even to the last moment when the words are uttered, *"he that is filthy, let him be filthy still,"* that person preferred the company of "dogs," sorcerers, or fornicators, or murderers, or idolaters or liars, or wrong-doers of some sort. *"The fearful, and unbelieving and abominable, and murderers and fornicators, and sorcerers and idolaters, and all liars shall have their part in the lake which burneth with fire and brimstone; which is the second death"* (21:8).

The first death is undone by Christ, who brings all the dead out of their graves; "Marvel not at this," the Lord says; for the hour is coming, in the which all that are in the graves shall hear His (Christ's) voice, and shall come forth; they that have done good, unto the resurrection of life; and they that have done evil, unto the resurrection of damnation." (John 5:28-29). Isaiah, Zechariah, Daniel and other of the Old Testament prophets prophesied of this same day. Daniel wrote: "Many of them that sleep in the dust of the earth shall awake, some to everlasting life, and some to shame and everlasting contempt" (Dan.12:2).

Then, in conclusion, in view of the dreadful fate of those whose names are not written in the book of life, a most impressive threat is added by the One who has never uttered an idle word, the One who is the very Word of God:

"I testify unto everyone that heareth the words of the prophecy of this book, If anyone shall add unto these things, God shall add unto him the plagues that are written in this book: And is anyone shall take away from the words of the book of this prophecy, God shall take away his part out of the book of life, and out of the holy city, and from the things which are written in this book. He which testifieth these things saith, Surely I come quickly."

> Do you "love His appearing?" (2 Tim.4:8).
> *Are you ready* for His appearing?
> Can you say from your hearts John's conclusion, *"Amen, Even so, come, Lord Jesus."*

If so, then, "The grace of our Lord Jesus Christ be with you all. Amen."

APPENDIX A

Those expositors, who believe in the literal sense of this chapter and these two witnesses are actual persons, are divided in the view whether they are Enoch and Elijah or Moses and Elijah. A few have always held they are Elijah and John, and we agree with those of the last view. A sect called "Seekers" under Cromwell expected John, the apostle, to be the forerunner of the second coming of Christ. Our reasons are as follows.

First and mainly, we cannot otherwise understand John when he introduces himself as part of a vision which has not yet been fulfilled. He takes the book from the Archangel's hand, who has just announced *"there shall be no more delay"* of events not yet arrived. The angel clearly fixes John's taking the book and receiving a commission as occurring at the end of this dispensation, not as belonging to the time when he saw the vision on Patmos.

Secondly, the mysterious prophecy of Jesus Christ, *"If I will that he tarry till I come, what is that to thee"* (John 21:22) means *something*. Jesus never uttered idle words. No adequate explanation has been found unless it is in the teaching that John is not to die until Christ comes to translate His saints. If this thought necessitates the view that John must have been translated as Elijah and Enoch in order to return and suffer physical death, then we can only say no proof exists that John ever died. The rumor has always persisted that he did not. Sir William M. Ramsey says, "When history began for the Christians late in the second century, hardly any historical authorities later than the Acts of the Apostles remained. Also, the events of Christian history during a long period after A.D. 62 had perished from memory.

Thirdly, coming half-way between the law and the latest Old Testament prophets, John, an executor of judgments, might well represent both the law and the prophets while John is the best representative possible of the Gospel. These appear at the moment in history when the "mystery of God is finished," and Jewish and Gentile Christians form one body. It seems suitable that a representative of the Gospel as well as the law should be seen engaged in preparing for the Lord's return, particularly since both are Jews.

Fourth, the style John adopted at this place is historical rather than descriptive of a vision. This approach suits the thought he is telling something which concerns him as well as the abrupt introduction of the two witnesses. This impersonal manner of speaking of himself is like the disciple in his Gospel who spoke only of "that disciple whom Jesus loved."

Fifth, in his vision, an Archangel expressly told John he must "prophesy again." That Archangel does not appear at the spot where John receives his commission until the end of this dispensation. Therefore, these words cannot apply to John's writings within the first century of this dispensation.

Sixth, John finds the little book (roll), which he eats, very bitter in his stomach (Revelation 10:9-11). Receiving a roll (little book) and eating it is the commissioning of a prophet as well as the words of that commission spoken by the Angel (Ezekiel 3:1-3, Jeremiah 15:16). Nothing could have been sweeter to John, the apostle, who wept that no one was found worthy to break the seven seals of the great roll (Revelation 5:2-4) than this prophecy related to Christ's return to finish His redemption. Nothing could have been more bitter to the "Apostle of Love" than to be sent to execute judgments upon the wicked in preparation for that return.

Seventh, John saw himself descend from heaven to earth to take that roll from the angel's hand. The words should be translated: *"And I went away* (to earth) *unto the Angel, and said unto Him, Give me the little book."* John's previous statement translated, *"I saw another mighty Angel come down from heaven,"* in the original does not contradict the idea that John sees this action from heaven since the words mean properly "descending from heaven."

APPENDIX B

Concerning the Temple of Ezekiel's vision, *Smith's Bible Dictionary* expresses the commonly accepted view in the following language: "It is not a description of a Temple that ever was built or ever could be erected at Jerusalem, and can consequently only be considered as the *beau ideal* of what a Shemitic Temple ought to be. Notwithstanding its ideal character, the whole is extremely curious and shows what the aspirations of the Jews were in this direction." To this view we can only ask, "Why may not *all* prophecy be regarded in the same light that the destructive higher critics of the present day? For our part, if plain statements of Scripture can be reduced to the mere imaginings of dreamy men, then all respect is ended either for the men who so pervert Scripture or for the Scriptures themselves as is too often the case. Of course, we retain our respect for the Word of God.

We accept, therefore, the interpretation of such expositors as Baumgarten, who is quoted in the Introduction to Lange's commentary on Ezekiel. He argues: "When Israel as a nation is converted to God, how can and how dare they exhibit their faith and obedience otherwise than in the forms and ordinances which

Jehovah has given to this nation?" Might we add, particularly in view of this very prophecy of Ezekiel: "And is it not plain that only after this conversion will the whole law in all its parts receives that fulfillment always hitherto demanded in vain?" However, we cannot express, nor do we think it needful to express, our faith in the literal interpretation of the prophet Ezekiel in such extreme language as Baumgarten uses when he says: "The Church of God is to find its goal in the condition here seen and described by the prophet of Israel. At that goal, the Gentiles finally enter again into the community of Israel and find in the law of Israel their national statute-book according to the will of God." The Talmudists taught that "the exposition of this portion (Ezekiel 40-49), relating to the setting up of the Temple and its ceremonies at Jerusalem, would first be given in Messianic times." Suffice to say, when John appears to conduct the measuring of the Temple, altar and worshipers, we shall come to understand in full the mysterious portions of the prophecy of Ezekiel.

APPENDIX C

Several theories have been advanced about the Woman this "great sign" represents. Additional reasons are given below which we think prejudice alone could brush aside. Interpreting this "great sign" as a pictorial (this term is unfortunate for a description of one of John's visions, but we know of no better) representation of the fulfillment of the promise inherent in Genesis 3:15, *"I will put enmity between thee and the woman, and between thy seed and her seed; it shall bruise thy head, and thou shalt bruise his heel."*

As to the question of who this Woman is, the most frequent answer is: "The visible is the church of Christ, and the man-child is the invisible or the spiritual church. The spiritual church is not simply those professing to be Christians, but those who are heavenly-minded Christians." This woman, however, is "clothed with the sun" or Christ, the Sun of Righteousness," clothes her. No! She cannot be merely a professing, visible church contrasted with a spiritual body of believers.

Besides, the professing, visible church will have fallen at the time Christ comes. *"Let no man deceive you by any means: for that day* (when the Lord comes again) *shall not come, except there come a falling away first"* (II. Thessalonians 2:3). That fallen church is better represented in the "stars of heaven" which Satan casts to the earth (Revelation 12: 4). That church will not be clothed with the sun as the Woman is but clothed in darkness. This Woman is in painful toil to accomplish bringing the man-child into the world. The apostate church will not be doing a work like this when Christ comes. "Like" can only produce "like." A nominal, merely professing, worldly church can never give birth to a spiritual, unworldly church. At best, it could only persecute such a church out of its midst.

Others say the Woman represents the Virgin Mary and the dragon is Herod, who sought to slay the infant Jesus. The Woman's flight into the wilderness represents Mary's flight to Egypt. How absurd since Mary fled with the Child in her arms. The Child went into "the wilderness" as well, and it is nonsense to think of the literal Egypt of Mary's day as a wilderness.

Others claim the Woman represents Eve. From this standpoint, however, nothing can be made of the child-birth or the flight into the wilderness. Again, the

claim is made that the woman represents the Jewish church whereas the man-child represents the Christian church or Christ. We ask, "When has the Jewish church labored and toiled to bring the Christian church into being? Also, in what sense was the Jewish church "clothed with the sun" at Christ's birth? Did not this Mother, if the Jewish church, devour her Child Jesus in that she compassed His crucifixion by the Romans?[14]

---

14   Others would teach the Woman is the Christian Church and the Child, Jesus Christ. However, the Christian Church is the Child of

Why this persistent effort to make the Woman represent a church? Is it because of Paul's teachings regarding man's duty to his wife being the same as Christ's duty to His church? Or, is it because the word "church" happens to be a word of feminine gender? If for either or both reasons, then we ask: "When God began to fulfill this promise made to the woman in the garden of Eden by the birth of Jesus Christ (and His history since), did God recall that the Old Testament Israel or the Jewish church is represented as Jehovah's wife or bride just as in the New, the church is so represented? Did God recall the word "synagogue" is feminine in gender? On these two facts, did He think it a sufficient fulfillment of His promise to keep reference in some manner to the Jewish church as such? Or, did He judge that a promise made in the presence of a *literal woman*, Eve, must be fulfilled to a *literal woman*, Mary, since it was made in reference to woman as distinguished from man?

God most certainly *began* in the person of Jesus Christ to fulfill His promise in reference not just to woman but to literal womankind. Therefore, if this twelfth chapter of the Revelation is a symbolical representation of the fulfillment of the promise of Genesis 3:15, then the Woman of the "great sign" is womanhood—believing womanhood—not Eve alone, nor Mary. Above all, the "great sign" is neither the crucifying Jewish church nor the apostate church.

Furthermore, repeating in part what was said in chapter 8, we ask: "At what point during the Gospel dispensation is opportunity left for the fulfillment of Joel's prophecy quoted on the day of Pentecost and related to women prophesying except here? That prophesying certainly comes before the *"wonders in heaven above, and signs in the earth beneath."* If ever the Holy Spirit causes "your daughters" (Hebrew women) and "My handmaidens" (Gentile women) to prophesy, it must be during the dispensation which began at Pentecost with the outpouring of the Holy Spirit and closes when His restraining influence is removed (II. Thessalonians 2:7). Surely no one will claim this notable prophecy regarding women has yet been *filled out full*.

Other prophecies beside Joel's relate to the preaching of the Gospel, which certainly must take place before the Gospel ceases to be preached. To

mention but two: *"The Lord giveth the word; the women that publish the tidings are a great host"* (Psalm 68:11, R.V.). A distinct injunction is laid upon women to proclaim the deity of Jesus Christ and His lordship at the time of His second coming according to Isaiah 40: 9-10. The *Revised Version* corrects the grammar of the *Authorized*, reading: *"O thou woman that tellest good tidings to Zion, get thee up into the high mountain; "O thou that tellest good tidings to Jerusalem, lift up thy voice with strength; lift it up, be not afraid; say unto the cities of Judah, Behold your God! Behold the Lord God will come as a mighty one, and His arm shall rule for Him: Behold, His reward is with Him, and His work before Him."* Who

---

Christ, not His mother. (Hebrews 2:13).

is the "thou" addressed here? It cannot be Zion or Jerusalem or Judah who is addressed as "thou" since these are the ones to whom the good tidings are to be told.

Also, John the Baptist cannot be meant even though he is the subject of Isaiah 40: 3 because the person addressed in verses 9 and 10 is a female. Precisely the same reasons exist for translating "thou woman" here as "the women" in Psalm 68:11. One and the same prophecy is expressed in different forms as Dr. Adam Clarke long ago demonstrated. In each case of the two passages, the original is a feminine participle of the Hebrew verbal form *bisser*, "to tell good tidings."

Zechariah 14:7 reads: *"It shall be one day which shall be known to the LORD."* Dr. Chambers, author of *Lange's Commentary* on Ezekiel explains this verse as meaning: "The day shall be one in the sense of solitary, unique, peculiar. It is known to Jehovah; and by implication, to no one else in its true nature." This interpretation agrees with the teaching in the margin, which gives the reference, *"But of that day and hour knoweth no man, no, not the angels of heaven, but the Father only,"* (Matthew 24:36). Please look at the phrase preceding this one we have quoted from Zechariah. In the A. V., it reads, *"The light shall not be clear nor dark."*

Several ancient versions have, by a corruption of the text, rendered: "There shall not be light and cold and ice." Dr. Chambers translates, "It will not be light; the glorious shall withdraw themselves." The English Revisers read: "The light shall not be with brightness and with gloom." The American R.V. renders: "There shall not be light: the bright ones shall withdraw themselves." It is particularly to Dr. Chambers' rendering and the American R.V. that we would call attention. Who are these "glorious" or "bright ones?" This word is feminine plural, and it is precisely the word and form used in Psalm 45:9 rendered "honorable women." Kings daughters are among Thy honorable women."

Therefore, we see no obstacle in believing that the *"bright ones"* or "bright and/or shining women" are the same as the *"Woman clothed with the Sun"* of Revelation 12:1 since Zechariah is writing of precisely this period of time— unknown to anyone but Jehovah.

Mysterious as the matter may seem, no one who recalls Daniel 10:13 will doubt the way might need to be cleared by the man-child with Michael in opposition to the translation of the general body of saints. Furthermore, considering the awful fate which awaits women who pass through the Tribulation at Jerusalem (Zechariah14:2), we see a reason why Christian men as well as God Himself would assist their flight from the city. These *"honorable women"* will *"withdraw themselves"* and be borne away to the wilderness on the wings of the Great Eagle.

APPENDIX D

We do not think Scripture contains the teaching that any saints will be translated prior to the Tribulation and experience none of its trials. The Tribulation period divides into two distinct parts: (1) That which is the fruitage of unrestrained iniquity, culminating in the great world war of Revelation 9:13-21, and (2) That which is mainly the culmination of God's wrath *"against all ungodliness and unrighteousness of men,"* namely, the outpourings of the seven vials of wrath, chapters 15 and 16.

Because of the similarity of some of the features of judgments under the trumpets and under the vials, one is tempted to think these two series of troubles are the same events as to time under different aspects. It is often taught that way. A close inspection of the Scriptures has led us to quite another conclusion, namely, dividing the Tribulation into two distinct parts. The first set of judgments are man-inflicted by the wicked. The second set of judgments are God-inflicted. The reason they run along analogous lines in their features is because a principle of highest justice is always to punish in the line of offense committed. This principle is plainly annunciated under the third vial where God is justified in this angel's words: *"Thou art righteous, O Lord . . . because Thou hast judged thus . . . They have shed the blood of saints and prophets, and Thou hast given them blood to drink"* (16:5, 6).

That the judgments under the trumpets and under the vials are not synchronous seems proved by the three "Woe" trumpets. In each case, it is plainly declared that these are consecutive as to time (9:12; 11:14). Then, after the seventh trumpet just sounded, the twenty-four elders said, *"Thy wrath has come, and the time of the dead, that they should be judged, and that Thou shouldst give reward unto Thy servants . . . and shouldst destroy them that destroy the earth"* (11:18). The vials of destructive wrath are not due until after the seventh trumpet has sounded. This fact also proves the time for the reward of the righteous is not due either nor the resurrection of the dead until the seventh trumpet blows.

The translation of the righteous will take place under the seventh trumpet. Those who teach a pre-Tribulation rapture depend almost entirely upon the supposed teaching of Luke 21:36: *"Watch, ye therefore, and pray always, that ye may be accounted worthy to escape all these things that shall come to pass, and to stand before the Son of Man."* To whom was the Lord speaking? Mark 13:3 tells us Peter, James, John and Andrew received these words. Of course, we may say the words apply to all Christians whom these disciples represent. Yes, but can they apply to others while *excluding* those representatives to whom the words were spoken?

What became of these four disciples? James was put to death by Herod; and almost certainly, Peter was crucified according to John 21:19. Tradition teaches that Andrew was crucified also. Did the Lord intend us to infer these disciples perished because they did not watch and pray? Could they have "escaped all these things" had they watched and prayed? "NO" is the only answer we can give to these questions.

Therefore, the expression, *"all these things which shall come to pass,"* cannot apply to all the events prophesied by our Lord in Luke 21. The next question is, "To how many of the events does the expression apply?" We reply to certain events described in the parable of the fig tree, just preceding. The disciples must watch Tribulation events to the point, according to the parable, when the leaves of the fig tree *"shoot forth."* What the disciples are to watch and pray to escape is the *"summer"* which speedily follows and comes as a snare *"on all them that dwell on the face of the whole earth."*

This same time is spoken of in Revelation 3:10 as an *"hour of temptation, which shall come upon all the world, to try them that dwell upon the earth."* That hour is when the Lord comes *"as a thief."* As far as it applies to us personally, the time is when *"the spirits of demons working miracles go forth unto the kings of the earth and of the whole world, to gather them to the battle of that great day of God Almighty"* described in Revelation 16:14-15.

For the immediate disciples of the Lord, it meant an event partially fulfilling this prophecy—when Jerusalem was surrounded by the armies of Titus. At that time, a moment of escape from the beleaguered city enabled all the watching and praying Christians to escape the doomed city to Pella.

Daniel's words seem to agree with the view that all Jewish and Gentile Christians will pass through the first, or man-inflicted, part of the Tribulation: *"Go thy way, Daniel: for the words are closed and sealed up till the time of the end. Many shall be purified, and made white and tried; but the wicked shall do wickedly: and none of the wicked shall understand; but the wise shall understand"* (12:9-10). The teaching is not that the trials will sanctify but that the culmination of wickedness in its most awful features when restraint is removed will sober the careless among God's people. They will learn wisdom and turn to the Lord for cleansing while the wicked still pursue their calamitous way until God's wrath overtakes them.

Should the question be asked, "Who of all Christians are most certain to be honored by reigning with Christ during the Millennium?" The answer would be, "Those who were worthy of translation besides the apostles and the martyrs."

Revelation 20:4 gives some definite information on this point. In 12:17, we learn that Satan's object in raising Antichrist (ch.13) is to *"make war"* with those who *"hold"* (R.V.) *the testimony of Jesus"* while *20:4 tells us those "that were beheaded for the testimony of Jesus,"* will live and reign with Christ a thousand years.

Furthermore, this same verse informs us that those who reign with Christ are distinguished by the fact they *"had not worshipped the beast, neither his image, neither had received his mark upon their foreheads, or in their hands,*" and Revelation15:2-5 shows us this same body as raptured saints. In fact, these two classes, and none others most certainly lived when the Beast ruled and were raised to such honor. We cannot understand how "those who are left behind to endure the reign of Antichrist," can be represented as unspiritual persons who failed their highest privileges. Rather, Revelation 20:4 proves the comparatively late period for the general translation after the rapture of the man-child.

APPENDIX E

Our reasons for interpreting the man-child of Revelation 12 as the 144,000 sealed Israelites of Revelation 7 are as follows:

(1) Isaiah 66:7, 8 calls "a nation" a "man-child" and doubtless refers to this same event in history. Note it expressly says Zion brought forth before or "as soon as" it travailed. In Revelation 12, the teaching is quite the contrary, for the Woman travails while Satan watches for the outcome. Hence, this Woman is not representative of Zion. Zion's travail at the moment of or just after the birth of the man-child may refer to the earthquake which occurs following `the rapture.

(2) It is expressly declared the child is a male. However, the 144,000 on Mt. Zion with the Lamb in chapter 14 are, I believe, one and the same with the man-child. According to Weymouth's translation, verse 4 should be rendered "virgins" who *"have not defiled themselves with women."*

(3) When this male child ascends to heaven, Michael appears; and a great war with Satan follows. In the book of Daniel, it is prophesied concerning the time of this same great Tribulation as follows: *"At that time shall Michael stand up, the great prince which standeth for* (defends) *thy people* (that is, the Jews; Daniel was a Jew) . . . a*nd at that time thy people shall be delivered* (from this Tribulation), *everyone that shall be found written in the book."* Michael is nowhere mentioned in the Bible after Daniel except by Jude, who says he contended for the body of Moses, until this scene in Revelation 12 nor is he ever mentioned again. If Michael "stands up" for this male child, then the fact seems to prove the child is Jewish.

(4) Paul reminds us, "In the days when God shall judge the secrets of men by Jesus Christ," the order in which it will be done is as follows: "Tribulation and anguish, upon every soul of man that doeth evil, of the Jew first, and also to the Gentile; but glory, honor, and peace, to every man that worketh good, to the Jew first, and also to the Gentile" (Romans 2:16, 9, 10). In other words, when Christ assigns "glory, honor and peace" to His faithful, believing ones, He will reward the Jew first. What greater glory can Christ award than translation or resurrection upon which all the after-glory depends? This child being "caught up" is a scene of translation where "the Jew first" must be the order.

(5) Again, the 144,000 are called in 14:4, *"first-fruits unto God, and to the Lamb."* We ask, which first-fruits? According to Leviticus 23:10 and 17, two first-fruits were offered. The second first-fruits offering was made fifty days later than the first first-fruits offer-

ing. Since the order is *"the Jew first"* and *also the Gentile,"* the first-fruits offered *first* must be Jewish.

www.ingramcontent.com/pod-product-compliance
Lightning Source LLC
LaVergne TN
LVHW011205080426
835508LV00007B/615